Auditing Your Customer Service

The foundation for success

John Leppard and Liz Molyneux

London and New York

First published 1994
by Routledge
11 New Fetter Lane, London EC4P 4EE

Simultaneously published in the USA and Canada
by Routledge
29 West 35th Street, New York, NY 10001

© 1994 John Leppard and Liz Molyneux

Typeset in Times by Solidus (Bristol) Limited
Printed and bound in Great Britain by
Biddles Ltd, Guildford and King's Lynn

British Library Cataloguing in Publication Data

A catalogue reference for this book is available from the British Library.

Library of Congress Cataloging in Publication Data has been applied for

ISBN 0–415–09732–0

Contents

Figures and tables

FIGURES

TABLES

Foreword

In today's competitive climate many companies are finding that any advantages they try to establish through their core products and services are quickly eroded as they are mimicked by others. Since leadership by such means is becoming increasingly transitory, companies are seriously looking at other strategies by which to differentiate themselves from their competitors. High on their new agenda is customer service.

This book is designed to explore some of the key ideas behind customer service in an easy-to-read format, which never loses sight of the total marketing concept. What makes it particularly useful are the exercises which are provided after each chapter. These allow the reader to audit his or her organisation's customer service in a number of quite specific ways.

Although this book will be most helpful to less experienced marketers, their more experienced marketing contemporaries will certainly find something of value in these pages, as will inquisitive and forward-looking managers from other functional disciplines.

This is a timely and essentially practical contribution to one of the biggest challenges facing marketing over the next few years; that of providing quality customer service. It should help many companies to get started on a difficult road which will ultimately lead to success.

Martin Christopher
Professor of Marketing and Logistics
Cranfield School of Management

— *Preface*

In the pioneering days of the American wild west, the travelling salesman would go from town to town selling patent medicine. It was claimed that this elixir would cure all known bodily ills, from baldness to gout. Of course, it never did.

Today a new curative is on offer. Like its predecessor, this too, it is claimed, can do wonderful things. It can rejuvenate any flagging company and restore it to good health. The name of this miracle cure? Customer service.

Let us hasten to add that we are all in favour of customer service; it is just that we are not entirely happy about the way it is being sold. Like price, product, promotion or place, by itself customer service will achieve nothing. It is simply another piece of the marketing jigsaw puzzle that the company has to fit into place. In that sense it is no more nor any less important than any of the other pieces. While it can embellish good products or services, customer service can never rescue poor ones. Yet such is the growth of interest on the topic, we believe, that in many organisations the customer service tail is trying to wag the marketing dog.

One of the reasons for writing this book was therefore to redress the balance and provide a perspective on customer service within the total context of marketing.

Another reason that prompted us to write is that, in a large number of organisations, providing customer service is seen to be solely the responsibility of those few staff who actually come into contact with customers. For the majority of their colleagues, customers appear to be merely an abstract concept. Indeed, in our experience, some of these people are hard pushed even to describe who their customers are.

To our way of thinking, no company can claim to be 'customer focused' or 'customer led' until every function and department within the organisation genuinely believes that customers are important. It is to that end that we have written this book, hoping that it will be equally accessible to marketers and non-marketers alike.

It was also our intention that the reader should be able to connect the text with his or her company situation by completing the exercises at the end of each chapter. In this way, useful data can be assembled and should provide valuable insights regarding how and where improvements might be made.

Above all, we hope that this book will provide some new perspectives on the important area of customer care and that your 'audit' leads to greater success.

John Leppard and Liz Molyneux
Cranfield, December 1993

1 *What is customer service and why is it important?*

Stop half a dozen people at random in the street and ask them to define 'customer service'. As like as not there would be six different responses.

The stressed salesman who is already late for an important meeting would snap in reply something about 'trains not running on time and not being able to find a cab when one needs it'. The proud mother who is seeking an outfit for the fast-approaching wedding of her daughter would probably say, with considerable feeling, 'Having shop assistants who listened and didn't try to fob you off with garments which are obviously unsuitable.' The elderly couple who have just spent some hours waiting to be treated in the out-patients' departments of the local hospital would no doubt volunteer, 'Having appointment times honoured and not being messed about' – need we go on?

As these comments clearly illustrate, customer service can mean different things to different people, according to their circumstances. It is interesting to note that none of our random sample complained about not being extolled to 'Have a nice day', by someone wearing an artificial smile. So, what is customer service and why is it important?

In order to find out the answers to these questions it will be important to have a brief look at one of the central themes of marketing, the marketing mix.

THE MARKETING MIX

In essence, the marketing mix is the recipe which enables the company to reach its customers and build a successful business. As

Figure 1.1 The nature of the marketing mix

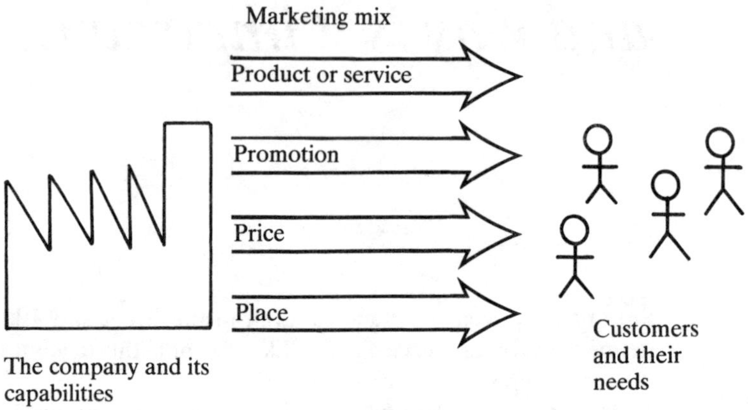

Figure 1.1 shows, it is the flexible coupling which aims to get the right product or service to the right place, in a way that it is required, at the right price. This often-quoted formula for success has become something of a litany for the marketer. The four 'Ps' (as product, promotion, price and place have become known) provides a neat, simple and easy-to-remember shorthand for the marketing mix. Just as a paint machine can mix various pigments in calculated proportions in order to match up with a particular colour on a chart, so can the components of the marketing mix be blended to meet different shades of customer needs. Indeed, achieving this is one of the major tasks facing the marketer.

The marketing mix blended for each market segment or group of customers should represent the best strategy for making impact and achieving the company's objectives.

Unfortunately, the four Ps concept often proves to be too general when it comes to the realities of marketing. Also it can lead to a narrow and far too blinkered approach to the marketing mix, which doesn't fully exploit some of the options open to the marketer. This is because each of the four Ps can in turn be broken down into a number of subactivities, each of which might be of greater or lesser importance for a particular company and its markets. Table 1.1 indicates some of the possible activities and provisions.

Table 1.1 Some of the subactivities under the four Ps umbrella

Product/service	Promotion	Price	Place
Design	Advertising	Discounts	Location
Quality	Personal selling	Credit loans	Delivery
Packaging	Sales promotions	Instalments	Transport
Range	Publicity	Commissions	Channels
Features	POS displays	Delayed payment	Stockholding
Benefits	Word of mouth	Direct debit	Order speed
Branding	Telesales		
Guarantees	Direct mail		
Backup (e.g. maintenance)	Catalogues		

By taking this expanded view of the marketing mix it becomes possible to examine customer transactions in more detail. Thus the customer who seeks to buy, let's say a car, might have some explicit requirements such as size, price and colour. However, there will also be some implicit needs which will influence that customer's choice. These might include factors like design, comfort, safety, economy in use, ease of servicing and so on. Therefore, while to an uninterested observer the transaction is only about buying a car, the customer in fact buys a whole product package consisting of the car itself and a number of other surrounding items some of which might be intangible.

As Figure 1.2 shows, the product/service package can range from 100 per cent tangible (the left of the spectrum) to 100 per cent intangible (the right-hand end). In all probability few products or services are likely to feature at the extreme ends, although, as the illustration shows, some get very close. For example, a commodity item such as coal might have minimal intangible features and be positioned at point A on the spectrum. Something like a car might be at point B. Perhaps a cosmetic or glamour item would figure at point C. Even something as intangible as, say, a counselling service, might have a tangible element like a question-naire or a list of action points and for this reason appear at point D on the spectrum.

The problem facing the marketer is to understand how to put together the most attractive product (or service) package without

Figure 1.2 The tangible/intangible package spectrum

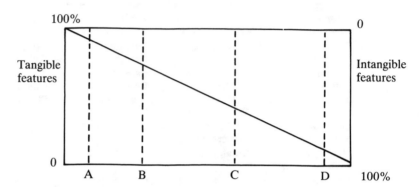

incurring astronomical costs. Clearly every item in the so-called 'product surround' involves an element of cost, yet not all items are necessarily valued to the same extent by the customers. For example, with cars some groups might be prepared to pay more for added safety features, whereas others would pay extra for speed and performance.

Indeed, the current issue about better locks for cars illustrates the marketer's dilemma. With an ever-increasing number of car thefts the police and consumer groups are calling for thief-proof locks. This does not provide an insurmountable technical problem and better security could certainly be provided ... but at a cost. At present all manufacturers seem to be wary of making the first move for fear of making their product less competitive at a time when money is tight.

A technique for evaluating the competitive merits of various features of the product is explained later in Chapter 2 (p. 28). For now it is enough to recognise that the product element of the four Ps does in fact really mean a whole product package which appeals to both the explicit and implicit needs of customers.

In a similar way the promotional 'package' can provide hard information which helps the prospective buyer, but it can equally work at a more subjective level, such as creating expectations or building up confidence.

Price, as we know, carries with it connotations of quality and exclusiveness. Upmarket products which are priced low send out mixed messages to customers and make them wary. Conversely, patently poor-quality products which are priced high simply remain to gather dust of the shelf. Also, within the pricing element of the marketing mix is the facility to make the financial transaction as painless as possible for the customer, by offering suitable discounts or arranging special methods of payment.

The place element of the marketing mix is concerned with the product or service being available to customers as and where they prefer to receive it. This area is therefore mainly concerned with inventory and logistics. It would be exceedingly foolish to have a world-beating product if, when a customer wants it, it is out of stock. Yet common sense tells us that there has to be a compromise between the stock levels that the company can afford to hold and the demands of the customers.

SUCCESSFUL COMPANIES SATISFY THEIR CUSTOMERS

 Successful companies are those who by accident or design have managed to get their marketing mix right for particular groups of customers. Moreover, they manage to do this consistently over time.

In the examples given at the beginning of this chapter it can now be seen that the organisations in question had in fact failed to manage the marketing mix properly. The railway had not met the customer's expectation of arriving at his destination on time. Thus its product quality was at fault. Similarly, the cab company did not have enough vehicles on the ground. The dress shop didn't hold the appropriate stock and the hospital could not deliver its consultancy on time.

If these situations were to continue unchecked, and if they had a choice, then the disgruntled customers who featured in our random sample would vote with their feet and take their custom elsewhere. Such is the reality of business life in an increasingly competitive environment.

Recognising this, and breaking out of the mind-set that the over-simplified notion of the four Ps sometimes produces, many companies are starting to redefine their marketing mix. For example, a manufacturer of men's aftershaves and toiletries has defined its marketing mix as shown in Figure 1.3. In other words, the four Ps in reality becomes five Ps and two As.

Figure 1.3 Marketing mix for men's toiletries

Figure 1.4 Marketing mix for plastic mouldings

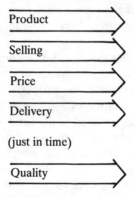

Alternatively, another company supplying plastic moulded products to computer manufacturers finds that its marketing mix is as shown in Figure 1.4. The mnemonic made from the initial letters of this particular mix sums up the business very accurately.

'*P*lease *S*end *P*retty *D*amn *Q*uick'

It can be noted that the second company had no need for advertising, publicity and packaging, unlike the first one. It, therefore, tailored the mix accordingly.

CUSTOMER SERVICE AND THE MARKETING MIX

It can now be seen that an astutely managed marketing mix not only ensures that the company stays highly competitive, which in the long-run means profitable, but also that it gets as close as possible to meeting the expectations and needs of customers.

In this sense, whenever the marketing mix is mismanaged the customer experiences it as a fall in service. As we observed in the earlier examples, from the customer's point of view the short-comings can stem from poor quality, late delivery, lack of choice or design or whatever. Just as one ingredient missing from a recipe can render the final cooked dish inedible, so can a substandard element of the true marketing mix alienate otherwise interested potential customers.

Thus at one level customer service can be defined as the quality of the cake which is set before the customer. However, the concept of customer service has to be stretched further than this to include the 'icing on the top' as well.

The reason that companies are paying so much attention to this extra decorative finish is that in many businesses products and services have become almost indistinguishable from those against which they compete. Moreover, within a narrow band, prices are also likely to be similar. The same goes for promotion and place. Therefore, in order to differentiate themselves, companies strive to add something extra to their transactions with customers. The world of politics has an apposite expression for this difficult to define extra ingredient. There it is called the 'feel good factor'. Such is the power of this that regardless of policy manifestos and the like, the feel good factor among voters can swing the outcome of an election.

In the business world the feel good factor is generated by the customer being treated with courtesy and attention at all points of their contact with the company. It is the customer feeling that he or she is important and that the person with whom they are dealing is pulling out all the stops on their behalf. It is the warm feeling which stays with the customer and makes him or her act as a sales-person on your behalf, by recommending your company to friends and relatives.

It is not easy to build up an organisation which is committed to making customers 'feel good'. It takes only one surly employee behaving in a slip-shod manner to destroy all the effort and hard work invested in the enterprise. To operate at this new high standard is more than a flavour of the month gimmick; it requires application and determination to put the customer first in the minds of everyone from the boardroom down.

CARE FOR EXISTING CUSTOMERS

Read almost any book on marketing or management and either explicitly or implicitly it will describe the purpose of 'the business' as being 'to create and keep customers'. Thereafter most books go on to focus solely on the issue of winning customers. It is as if it is believed that keeping them will happen automatically. Not only is such an attitude dangerously complacent, it is also far from the truth.

Moreover, it is estimated that it can cost as much as five times more to win a new customer than it does to get repeat business from an existing one. In industries where the value of the product or service is high and the purchasing frequency low, the relative cost between doing business with new or existing customers can be nearer ten to fifteen times higher. For example, some research in the car industry has shown that it can cost seventeen times as much to attract new customers as it does to keep existing ones.

Another piece of research by Reichheld and Sasser[1] has shown how customer retention can have a dramatic impact on profits (see Table 1.2). As this shows the impact of customer retention varies

Table 1.2 Profit increase vs customer retention

Industry	Profit increase for a 5 per cent increase in customer retention (per cent)
Mail order	20
Auto service chain	30
Software	35
Insurance brokerage	50
Credit card	125

[1] F.F. Reichheld and W.E. Sasser Jr, 'Zero defections: quality comes to services', *Harvard Business Review*, September–October 1990.

from one type of industry to another. Nevertheless, even with what some might consider to be a modest increase in customer retention rates, the payback in profits can be fourfold or perhaps many times more.

It therefore clearly pays to consider one's business as concerned with developing relationships as opposed to simply sales trans- actions. Once this conceptual leap has been made, the issue of customer loyalty is no longer an abstract piece of jargon to be bandied about at board meetings. Instead, it becomes a central strategic concern for those charged with safeguarding the future of the company. However, customer loyalty is not achieved at one fell swoop; relationship-building has to go through a number of stages as shown in Figure 1.5.

The customer loyalty chain starts with prospects who, one would like to think, were well-chosen. The salesperson converts the prospect into a customer, who perhaps can be regarded as more of a regular customer as repeat purchases are made. Eventu- ally such is the relationship that even when pressured by competi- tors the customer continues to support your company. The ultimate destination of the relationship is for it to reach a stage where the customer becomes an advocate for your product or service. At this level he or she will recommend your company quite unsolicited, in effect becoming a valuable sales asset.

In order to develop such a chain it is essential that the end result, customer loyalty, is considered right from the very beginning. Thus there is no room for sales staff who use deceit or bullying tactics as their stock-in-trade to 'win' customers. While

Figure 1.5 The customer loyalty 'chain'

Prospect ⟶ Customer ⟶ Regular Customer ⟶ Supporter ⟶ Advocate

Main organisational concern is to 'net' customers

Main organisational concern is to keep customers by developing an ever-improving relationship with them

Conceptual gap

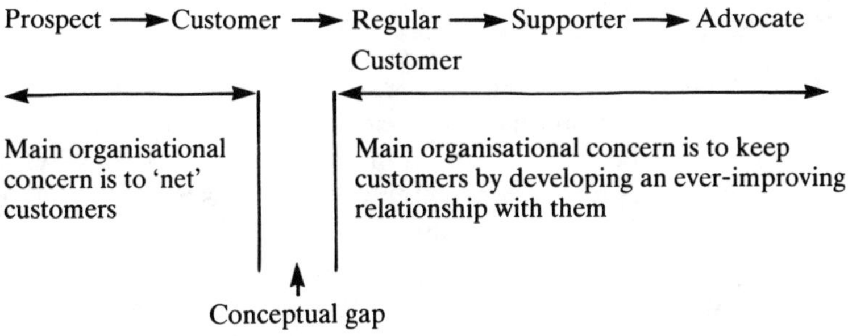

Figure 1.6 The conversion pyramid

they might achieve their short-term sales targets, they are actually undermining any prospects the company might otherwise achieve in long-term profitability. Indeed, the success of the company at relationship-building could be monitored by assessing the conversion rate at each stage of the chain. In this way a conversion 'pyramid' can be built up as shown in Figure 1.6. Just as not every prospect will be converted into a customer, so there will be a 'drop-out' rate at each stage of the customer loyalty chain. So, for example, if it was found that very few customers entered into further transactions, then that raises some very contentious issues regarding the quality of the product or how the company is perceived in general. Consideration of what gives any company's conversion pyramid its distinctive shape can help to identify where the energy and resources for improving relationship-building might be best invested.

MODES OF CUSTOMER SERVICE

As Figure 1.7 demonstrates, the customer service comes from providing, in terms of our earlier analogy, both the cake and the icing, where both are of a sufficiently high quality. In most businesses to have one without the other is not enough to succeed.

 Companies who invest in so-called customer service programmes when their basic customer package is sadly lacking are only flattering to deceive. As the old saying goes 'they might

Figure 1.7 Modes of customer service

		Low	High
'Feel good factor'	High	Sham	Winner
	Low	Loser	Honest striver
		Low	High

Quality of the basic package

fool some of the people some of the time', but this is not a formula for long-lasting success.

The company which gets its product or service package right will already have a head start over many of its competitors. It can become an out and out winner if in addition to this it can develop the feel good factor in its customers.

SUMMARY

Customer service can mean different things to different people. For this reason it is important that the company is clear about what it is trying to achieve with 'customer care' programmes and their like. Worthwhile approaches to customer service are unlikely to succeed as stand-alone activities, because they need to be set within the context of an overall marketing strategy. In turn, this means that the company knows who its customers are, what needs they have, and how an integrated marketing mix can be formulated to make an impact on each specific market segment.

Objectives of C.E.P.

In essence, this means that the company offers a product or service designed to meet customer needs, together with all the intangible elements which go with it ... including customer service.

It is eminently sensible to make customers feel good about their dealings with the company. Not only will this help to win them in the first place, but it also contributes to establishing the foundations of a longer-term relationship. As was indicated, the profit potential to be derived from retained customers makes relationship building an extremely fruitful task.

However, since the orientation of many companies has been concerned mainly with winning new customers, this shift in emphasis to customer retention often needs to be accompanied by new staff attitudes. The modes of customer service matrix showed clearly how successful companies distance themselves from their contemporaries by getting the basic package *and* the feel good factor right.

The remainder of this book will examine how to audit and improve both of these elements of customer service and indicate what the implications might be for the organisation. However, before progressing further, here are some questions and exercises to help you to discover where your company stands at present in terms of customer service.

By completing the following materials you will be generating useful information about your company, not only about its strengths but also what might need to be changed.

EXERCISE 1.1 SOME QUESTIONS TO BE ASKED

1 How important is service in your particular type of business?

2 Is your concept of service based on opinion or has it been researched in order to find out what it is that customers expect of you?

3 On balance do you think you can make more impact on customers by:
a) Improving the tangible product/service 'package'? or
b) Improving the service element, the intangible part?

4 What percentage of your business is repeat purchases?
a) Could this be improved?
b) What would have to be done differently to bring about improvements?

5 In what ways can you create the feel good factor for your company (for example, better handling of enquiries)?

6 Do you believe that there is the right 'climate' in your company for providing a high level of customer service?
   a) If there is, what factors in particular make the greatest contributions to achieving that climate?
   b) If there isn't, what organisational factors need to change in order to get the right climate?

7 If you could wave a magic wand, which three things would you wish to change in order to improve your organisation's approach to (or level of) customer service?
   a) What attempts have you made in the past to bring about these changes?
   b) If you have tried before why were you not successful?
   c) Having learned from your earlier experiences, or coming new to the situation, what can you now do to
      i) bring about these changes yourself? or
      ii) influence important others to make these changes happen?

EXERCISE 1.2 CUSTOMER SERVICE – THE CORPORATE AUDIT

OBJECTIVE This exercise takes a broad look at the organisation in terms of the importance it attaches to customer service. In doing this, it raises some general issues about where things might be improved, particularly the contribution made by various functional areas of the company.

PROCEDURE Score this audit as follows:

0	1	2	3
Not true for our company	Sometimes true for our company	Often true for our company	Always true for our company

1 The organisation's mission statement mentions 'customer service' as being part of its special character.

2 Top management is involved and actively interested in customer service.

3 The general organisational climate is supportive of providing good quality customer service.

4 Top management is receptive to ideas about improving customer service.

5 People are clear about how they can raise and progress any good ideas they might have about customer service.

6 Staff get a fair hearing when they raise issues about customer service to top management.

7 Customer service is on the agenda of most management meetings.

8 The company provides regular training sessions or exercises to reinforce the importance of customer service.

9 The company actively encourages communication and the cross-fertilisation of ideas about customer service between (score only where applicable):

   a) Different levels of the organisation

   b) Different functional departments

   c) Different operating units

   d) Different international markets.

10 Overall the level of customer service and the general attitude towards it provided by these departments is satisfactory

   a) Production

b) Personnel ☐

c) Accounts/Finance ☐

d) Marketing/Sales ☐

e) Administration ☐

f) Other functional areas (name them):

_____ ☐

_____ ☐

11 Our record of introducing improvements in customer service is satisfactory. ☐

12 Every employee is aware of the high level of importance that the company attaches to customer service. ☐

TOTAL ☐

Customer service – Corporate audit: scoring and interpretation

This questionnaire reflects a number of factors that one would expect to be in place in a company dedicated to taking customer service seriously.

Not all the questions will be appropriate to every organisation. Although, for example, some may not have different operating units, and others may have different functional departments to those listed, none the less the questionnaire can be tailored to fit most situations.

Scoring

1 Add up the number of questions actually used. (Remember you are allowed to leave out those not applicable, and you might have added specific functional areas.)

2 Multiply this number by three to arrive at the *maximum* possible score.

3 Add up all points you allocated to arrive at the *actual* score.

4 Calculate the actual score as a percentage of the maximum (i.e., actual / maximum × 100).

Interpretation

100–90%   Your organisation is clearly taking customer service very seriously and ought to be reaping some rewards from doing so.

89–75%   Although you are in the top quartile of scoring, there is still room for improvement.

74–50%   You are above average but cannot be complacent because there is considerable scope for improvement.

49–25%   This is a very low score, and certainly indicates that much needs to be done to improve customer service.

Below 24%   Oh dear!

EXERCISE 1.3 CUSTOMER SERVICE – THE DEPARTMENTAL AUDIT

OBJECTIVE This exercise can follow on from Exercise 1.2 or be used in its own right. It is meant to be used in a specific department or functional area of the business. By using this questionnaire it becomes possible to compare how different departments respond to providing customer service.

PROCEDURE

0	1	2	3
Not true for our company	Sometimes true for our company	Often true for our company	Always true for our company

1 The department understands how it can contribute to customer service. ☐

2 The general climate of the department is supportive of customer service. ☐

3 The senior manager(s) of the department take a proactive role in matters concerning customer service. ☐

4 The department's general record for providing customer service is satisfactory. ☐

5 The number and quality of new ideas about customer service provided by this department are satisfactory. ☐

6 Customer complaints received by the company do not reflect badly on this department. ☐

7 This department has taken steps to improve its customer service activities. ☐

8 There is an on-going action plan for improving customer service. ☐

9 Staff are highly motivated with regards to providing customer service. ☐

10 Staff are encouraged to contribute new ideas regarding customer service. ☐

TOTAL ☐

Scoring

The maximum score is 30. Calculate your actual score as a percentage of this (i.e., actual score / 30 × 100).

Interpretation

100–90%   This department is clearly taking customer service very seriously and should be seen as a major contributor to the company efforts.

89–75%   This department is in the top quartile of scoring, but there is still room for improvement.

74–50%   You are above average but cannot be complacent because there is considerable scope for improvement.

49–25%   Unless this is an initial survey to find out about customer service (in which case it represents the starting-point), scores in this quartile are not very good and cannot be justified.

Below 24% Unless a convincing argument can be put forward regarding why this department has nothing to contribute to customer service, such a low score reflects an extremely poor response.

2 *Identifying your customers and their needs in order to get the basic product or service right*

As was shown in Chapter 1, without first having a competitive product or service to offer the market, any investment in customer service will be merely a distraction and a mis-direction of resources. Rather like house construction, customer service has to be built on sound foundations. No amount of cosmetic tampering can disguise the fact if the product or service does not perform adequately in the first place.

This chapter will look at how to get products or services tailored more accurately to meet customer needs and thereby provide the prerequisite for a successful customer service programme. It must be stressed that for the purposes of the structure of this book we have quite deliberately separated work on the basic product and service from work on the service element of the customer package. In real life it would be more likely that both issues would be tackled simultaneously as and when opportunities were provided to do so.

CUSTOMER SEGMENTATION

One of the biggest mistakes supplying companies make is to treat their customers as if they were all the same. This is patently not true and like the population at large, they come in all shapes and sizes, ages, from different walks of life and parts of the world. However, the corollary to this approach, to treat every customer as an individual case, would be a luxury, the cost of which would put it beyond the reach of all but a few businesses.

The solution to this apparent conundrum is to group customers into what are termed market segments. While on the surface market segmentation appears to be a fairly straightforward process, in practice it can often present problems. For this reason there is no easy prescription to follow, yet it goes without saying that the more astutely a company can segment its customers into different groups, the greater are the prospects of offering the right products or services to the right people.

Since the way the segmentation is done can be the key to future success or failure, it is worth spending a little time looking at some of the possible bases for the process. Although in truth it could be claimed that there are hundreds of ways of segmenting customers, in essence there are only three distinctly different approaches to guide one's analysis.

1 Segmentation on the basis of what is bought

This is perhaps the easiest and most obvious method of segmentation. Its main advantage is that it can make use of customer information which more often than not is readily available within the company. As Figure 2.1 illustrates, if a firm of solicitors used this approach they might find that they had four market segments: conveyancing, marital, wills and probate, and commercial contract work.

By analysing past sales records and considering the make up of the population in its 'catchment area', this firm ought to be able to allocate its resources along these lines. It would also develop its expertise in each area and thereby manage and sustain growth. By concentrating all its efforts into just these four products/segments the company progresses along its learning curve rapidly and can

Figure 2.1 Example of segmentation by products (a solicitor)

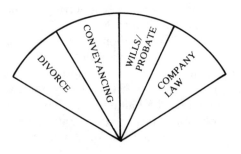

capitalise on the professionalism it brings to each area.

In a similar way a company might instead choose to segment its customer base by volume, outlets, geographical location, features or physical characteristics of the products, order size and so on. All of these considerations are a reflection of what is bought.

2 Segmentation on the basis of who buys

Here the spotlight switches from what is bought to the buyers themselves. With this approach new criteria come into play, for example, personality types, socio-economic groups, brand loyalty and demographic factors such as age, sex, etc. The underlying premise here is that knowing who buys enables the supplier to tailor the product or service more specifically. Another benefit is that the company can seek out more buyers who conform with the segment stereotypes.

In Figure 2.2 the example is that of a company which makes plastic drainpipes and guttering for buildings. It found that the architects were interested in new designs and specially made items. The local authorities needed products that were practical, robust and required minimum upkeep. Builders' merchants wanted bulk deliveries at very short notice. Moreover, these would have to be packed for easy transport and storage using fork-lift trucks. The DIY enthusiasts need small quantities, capable of being transported by car, together with very clear instructions about installation.

However, in order to be aware of the needs of these different segments the company had to monitor representative samples from

Figure 2.2 Example of segmentation on the basis of who buys (plastics company–building products)

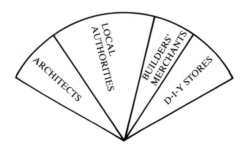

each one. In this way the company could assess the extent to which current products met existing needs, and also how these needs were changing over time. Internal sales records, useful though they were, could no longer provide all the necessary information. A conscious effort to go out and seek information had to be made.

3 Segmentation on the basis of why the customer buys

Here the focus is on understanding the customer's motivation for buying and to determine groups who are similar in their inclinations. Figure 2.3 shows how a car manufacturer might segment his customer base.

In this example it can be seen that for the segment concerned with safety, those features need to be enhanced and brought to prominence. For the 'economy' segment the emphasis will reflect efficient engine design, running costs, standardised servicing at long intervals and so on. The 'image and status' segment will be more concerned with the size, styling and exclusiveness of models, while the 'reliability' segment will want vehicles that will never let them down, regardless of the weather conditions or how they are garaged.

Of course this is only one method of differentiating customers. Approaches based on other aspects of personal motivation, such as benefits sought, attitudes to the product or service, customer preferences and so on, could be used to equally good effect if chosen perceptively.

In practice most companies will probably use a combination of these criteria rather than rely on just one of them. By doing this

Figure 2.3 Example of customer segmentation by personal motives (cars)

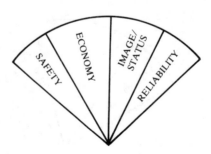

they can develop a more accurate description of each customer segment and thereby be better placed to provide products or services that have a high level of acceptability. Indeed, the more creatively the market can be segmented the greater are the prospects of the company developing some form of competitive advantage. Or to put it another way, if the company approaches the market in much the same way as everyone else, why should the customer see any difference?

From what has been said about segmentation it is self-evident that whereas grouping customers on the basis of what is bought is fairly simplistic, segmentation on the basis of 'who buys' and 'why' calls for a deeper and more sophisticated level of understanding of actual and potential customers.

THE 'ACID TEST' FOR A SEGMENT

As stated earlier, the members of any particular market segment should have a high degree of similarity with each other, while at the same time being distinctly different from other groups of customers.

However, there are also other considerations to bear in mind:

- A market segment should be sufficiently large as to offer the company a good return for its investment and effort.
- How the segment is described must be relevant to the purchasing decision.
- The segment must be reachable both in terms of communications and physical delivery.
- Would the segmentation of customers provide a competitive edge?

Sensible though these criteria might be, many companies have over-segmented. That is to say they are dealing (or attempting to deal) with too many segments. As a result they find that they are trying to be too many things to too many customers and hence their marketing focus, and with it customer service, becomes diluted.

As a rule of thumb, it is unlikely that a company can adequately service more than five or six market segments. Naturally enough these need to be of a sufficient size to sustain the business.

The issue of reachability is also one that is sometimes overlooked.

A senior executive of a financial services group was once heard to claim that his company had two market segments, 'Those customers who do business with us and those who don't'.

Instinctively one can sense that such a method of segmentation is not very workable, yet it does meet three out of the four criteria listed above. After all, the segments are large (especially those who don't do business with the company). It is 'related' to the buying decision and there is a distinct difference between the two segments. Having said that, how does one reach the 'yet to buy' segment? Who are they? Where are they? What do they read? What are their problems? The answers to these questions will clearly demonstrate that this group is by no means homogeneous and is therefore not a market segment. It will remain unreachable unless the segmentation is carried out in a more intelligent manner.

How a company segments its customers is so central to marketing that all subsequent transactions, including customer service, will be influenced by the decision. Too many companies tend to segment along fairly obvious lines and by doing so miss the opportunity to establish a competitive advantage. By doing what all the other companies do and not seeking a different angle or approach, they make themselves just one of the pack in the customers' eyes.

Thus the critical first step towards understanding customers' needs is to segment them. The most sensible means of doing this will depend upon the nature of the industry in which one operates. Thus, the criteria will vary from business to business – for some it might be geographical area, for others it could be product range, size of account, credit worthiness, method of delivery or collection and so on.

THE NEXT STEP

Having segmented the customer base it is useful to abandon all preconceived notions about how well you believe your product or service is received. Instead, question customers in each segment objectively and get their views about what they look for in the product or service and, just as important, how well your output matches their expectations. Of course, there might be some surprising answers which may lead to a redefinition of the earlier segmentation criteria. However, this is not necessarily a bad thing.

At the end of the day one is seeking to establish a competitive advantage and anything which leads in this direction can only be good news.

Clearly, nothing can be done to change the product range or service levels of competitors, but it is possible to concentrate on the performance of one's own output and do everything within reason to find ways of reaching or exceeding the standards required by customers. To this end it is useful to adopt an open-minded attitude about current practice and accept that nothing is so good that it cannot be improved.

In fact there should be little need to make too many assumptions about the customers' viewpoint because much valuable information will be available already. Throughout the company the various people who come into contact with customers possess a wealth of data. For example, sales representatives, people in accounts, delivery drivers, customer complaints, after-sales service personnel and so on, all have a partial picture of each customer. In addition to knowing some of their likes and dislikes they will also have developed strong perceptions about their contact companies. By drawing all of this information together into a central pool it becomes possible to establish a fairly accurate 'photo-fit' of each customer segment.

Unfortunately much of this valuable but informal customer information goes unheeded, so, for example, when a person leaves the company all of their customer knowledge goes with them. Rarely are such people requested to record a thumb-nail sketch of their customer contacts prior to their departure.

However, useful though this bank of anecdotal customer information is, it can also run the risk of being tainted by personal prejudice. For example, the comments of 'favourite' customers may be given undue weight in any internal discussions about products and services. Therefore, in order to achieve a higher level of objectivity many companies follow up all customer transactions with a questionnaire designed to highlight where and how customer satisfaction might be improved. Yet, as we all know, even questionnaires are not blemish-free. Designing them is a science in itself. All too often the well-intentioned amateur will cobble together an ill-conceived document full of leading or ambiguous questions. Not surprisingly, the end result of such enterprise can be misleading and sometimes even downright dangerous.

To achieve total objectivity it can be extremely useful to employ a third party to conduct research on your behalf. It is easy to see why. Just imagine that a sales representative was charged with obtaining information which could be construed to reflect poorly on his own level of performance. In such circumstances is it likely that the unvarnished truth will be relayed back? Just to ask the question is to know the answer.

If there are sufficient in-house resources this information gathering exercise could be conducted without recourse to an external agency, but it is wise to be aware of the pitfalls. If internal resources are used in order to save money, can the company be absolutely certain that the answers are truly objective? If they are that's excellent. If not, it could mean taking a massive gamble with the hard won budget. A third-party researcher with no axe to grind can discover the true position and pass on the findings 'warts and all', and, what is more, will have the experience gathered from conducting many previous projects such as this to fall back on.

There are plenty of market research companies around, but there are also some specialist customer service research companies and these are the ones which concentrate solely on such studies and therefore have wide experience of similar projects, not to mention the specially trained researchers necessary to conduct the interviews.

CHOOSING A RESEARCH COMPANY

As with any successful relationship, business or otherwise, each party must feel comfortable with the other. Perhaps at the end of the day this might be the most important factor in choosing an outside research company. However, it will be necessary to check that the company can also meet certain factual requirements that will have a bearing on the particular research project. Exactly how this might be done is illustrated in Exercise 2.2 at the end of this chapter.

Having talked to external research companies and selected the most appropriate one, the next step is to establish the project brief in detail.

Table 2.1 Information-gathering techniques – their strengths and drawbacks

Technique	Main strengths	Drawbacks
Desk research	Can provide quick results. Relatively cheap and controllable	Information might not be sufficiently specific leading to interpretation problems, or might be out of date
Company sales records	Readily accessible	Mainly historical and may not be in a readily usable form
Company financial records	Readily accessible	Mainly historical and may not be easily translated
Salesperson records	Readily accessible and current information	Interpreting narrative into quantifiable data can be difficult. Reporting might be inadequate
Journals, etc.	Relatively easy to obtain	Information is often too general
Trade association	Have good understanding of specific industries or sectors	Quality of information and degree of co-operation varies between trade associations
Government agencies or statistics	Vast amount of information reasonably accessible	Need to know way through the 'system'. Can be swamped with too much useless information
External research (in general)	Based on competitive environment, will be current and therefore provides confidence for decision-making	Can be costly/time consuming. Samples must be accurate. Can be difficult to organise

Source: After M.H.B. McDonald and J.W. Leppard, *The Marketing Audit*, Oxford: Butterworth-Heinemann 1991.

THE BRIEF

A brief enables the customer research company to appreciate the scope and details of the project. It has to embrace not only the obvious points that need to be elicited, but also any particular sensitivities there are felt to be in the market-place. The better the brief, the better the chance of the research company providing the information required. On receiving the brief, research companies will respond with a written proposal and usually provide a personal presentation to explain their methodology, feedback systems and justify their anticipated fees. Invariably, during this discussion phase the brief becomes more finely tuned.

Working closely with the chosen research company, one can define the number of interviews to be conducted and the style of interviewing which best suits the situation and time frame. For example, is it best that interviews are conducted by telephone, or face-to-face? Should be they conducted in a structured or semi-structured format?

There are advantages and disadvantages with every type of information-gathering approach as summarised in Table 2.1. It is important to be aware of the strengths and weaknesses of any proposed research method before agreeing upon its use.

HOW COMPETITIVE IS THE PRODUCT OR SERVICE?

The main thrust of any research, whether conducted internally or externally, is to establish the extent to which the product or service (a) meets customers needs and expectations and (b) compares with competitive offers.

Therefore the research has to generate information good enough to facilitate sensible analysis in these areas. Exactly what information might be required will clearly be dictated by the particular circumstances surrounding an individual product or service. However, by way of example, let us consider the following case-study. It concerns a company Ski Hi-Kites, whose main competitors are Buzzard and Tempest.

The first level of analysis will be to compare the competing products by listing their physical characteristics or features as shown in Table 2.2. Such an analysis will show at a glance how Ski Hi compares with the two main competitors on all of the salient features of equivalent products. However, as we saw earlier when

Table 2.2 Features comparison (example only)

	Ski Hi	*Buzzard*	*Tempest*
Height	100 cm	100 cm	90 cm
Width	60 cm	50 cm	50 cm
Weight	medium	lightest	heaviest
Materials	woven nylon	metallised plastic	clear plastic
Design	traditional	traditional	traditional
Length of lead	longest	shortest	medium
Stunting facility	yes	yes	no
Collapsibility/ storage	easy	easy	difficult
Cost	medium	cheapest	most expensive
Availability	toy shops	petrol stations	mail orders

Note: The names Ski Hi, Buzzard and Tempest have been invented for this case-study. As far as we know, no real companies so named exist. If they do, we trust that our example will cause no offence.

we looked at segmentation, customers do not buy a product for its features alone, but for the benefits it brings them. It is therefore possible to connect each feature with a possible benefit. A neat way of transposing one to the other is to use the expression 'which means that' as shown below.

- 'it is of low weight *which means that* you can launch it in the lightest breeze'
- 'our height to width ratio *means that* it is stable in flight'
- 'our use of woven nylon material *means that* it never tears'
- 'it has a traditional design *which means that* the kite can also be used for stunting'
- 'because our lead is longest it *means that* our kites out-soar all others'
- 'our metallised plastic *means that* the kite looks bright and impressive in the sky' and so on.

The characteristics of the kites can now be examined *not* in terms of what they are, but what they provide. Even so, what we have called 'benefits' are not genuine benefits unless they provide something the customer actually wants and would influence the purchase decision.

Table 2.3 Benefit comparison (example only)

	Benefits	Sky Hi	Buzzard	Tempest
	Ease of launching	2	1	3
Decreasing	Visual impact	3	1	2
importance	'Stuntability'	1	1	3
to customers	High flying	1	3	2
	Availability	2	1	3

Notes: 1 = best; 2 = next best; 3 = worst.

Now it can be seen why it is important to discover what it is that kite-buyers seek. Until the company is clear about what they value it can never tailor the product around their needs. If they want a long-lasting kite then perhaps it is right to use woven nylon material. In contrast, if the kite is seen only as a temporary plaything, then it might be 'over-engineering' it, since for such buyers this feature bestows no benefits whatsoever.

The earlier features comparison in Table 2.2 thus needs to give way to a benefits comparison as shown in Table 2.3. This gives an entirely different picture regarding the competitiveness of Sky Hi-Kites. It actually falls down on the two benefits which customers rate the highest.

DESIGNING A BETTER PRODUCT OR SERVICE

Staying with the kite example, it can be seen that any worthwhile investment in the product must address the issues of 'launching' and 'visual impact'. These are the areas most highly valued by customers and where Ski Hi lags behind its major competitor Buzzard. There are two possible improvement strategies open to the company. It could attempt to:

1   bring the specification more or less into line with Buzzard, i.e., reduce weight and change the construction material; or
2   leap-frog Buzzard by introducing innovations in this area.

Faced with options like these every company must make its own choice. Both in this example and in real life apeing the market leader is less risky, but at the same time does not create a competitive advantage. The alternative, to go for innovation, carries with it higher risks but also the prospect of higher rewards.

However, should a company choose to bite the innovation bullet then it needs to harness whatever creativity it can muster. It is a sad fact of management life that seniority and exalted position do not necessarily make a person more creative. Creative people do, on the whole, stay creative irrespective of their upward mobility. Far better then if the company tried to identify and track down the creative people in the organisation, and charged them with the task of coming up with new ideas. This can be accomplished by developing something akin to quality circles, but instead directed towards improving innovation. Alternatively there is a wide range of 'idea generating techniques'[1] which can be used. Whatever the chosen mechanism, the overriding concept will be to devise new product features which in turn will supply superior customer benefits.

If for a moment we let our imagination run riot on the above case-study, kite launchability might be improved by inventing some kind of launcher, or perhaps having a helium-filled balloon to lift the kite into the skies. The visual impact might be improved by using new materials, fluorescent colours which glow in the dark, trailing streamers, small replaceable canisters which leave a 'vapour trail' and so on.

Of course some ideas will be generated which will be prohibitive in terms of costs or technical feasibility, but if enough new ideas are put forward one or two of them are bound to be winners. The ultimate criterion will be that the product or service gains a genuine competitive advantage in its particular market segment.

Whatever improvements it is decided to introduce, they should above all be:

■ Practical and unambiguous.
■ Measurable (in terms of their impact on the market).
■ Communicable (to customers and company staff alike).

Over time, the enthusiasm and dedication the company shows to improving its products or services for the benefit of its

---

[1] The interested reader could go more deeply into the subject area by reading Simon Majaro, *The Creative Marketer*, Oxford: Butterworth-Heinemann 1991.

customers will develop a new atmosphere which transmits to customer care. There will be pride and satisfaction from knowing that only high standards are good enough. It is from this launch pad that the mission to improve customer service (and with it sales and profit margins) takes off.

SUMMARY

In this chapter we have looked at the need for the supplying company to provide a basic package, whether a product or a service, which meets its customers' expectations. By segmenting customers into distinctive groups which have needs and aspirations that are different from those of other segments, the company is better prepared to supply the right offer to the right people.

Simple though this sounds, in practice customer segmentation is not easy. One reason for this is that it can be approached in many different ways, and the company often chooses the easiest method, not the best. The second reason is that in order to segment for competitive advantage it is often necessary to know more about customers than is readily available from internal records.

Having segmented the customer base, it is then essential to monitor the extent to which the product or service meets the existing and changing needs of customers. However, this cannot be considered in isolation, but must be looked at in the context of options which are available in the market. While it is perfectly feasible for the company to research such situations itself by using its formal and informal sources of information, internal initiatives are often hampered by a lack of expertise or objectivity.

A case was put forward for using third-party professional researchers, but this in turn puts added obligations on the company to be clear about what it is trying to achieve. By using a third party the company cannot abdicate its responsibility, for it is charged with managing the relationship and bringing the results of the research to life in terms of improved products or services.

The search for objectivity and getting closer to meeting customer needs brings with it a subtle change in the organisational climate. By putting the customer first a new reality permeates the business and with it the desire to search for excellence in all transactions.

EXERCISE 2.1 CUSTOMER SEGMENTATION

OBJECTIVE This exercise enables a critique to be made about the current method of segmentation and provides pointers as to how it might be improved.

PROCEDURE

1 Describe how your customers are segmented at present. Make brief notes on a separate sheet. *Note*: if you don't know how your customers are segmented, try to find out before proceeding. If there is no clearly understood method of segmentation, write down how it might be done.

2 How well does this approach stand up to the 'acid test' of segmentation? Score each of the following criteria between 0–10, where 10 represents an unqualified 'yes'.
   Segments derived on the basis of 1 above.

   a) Can be clearly described individually. ☐

   b) Each represent a group of customers with a high level of homogeneity. ☐

   c) Are distinctly different from each other. ☐

   d) Are sufficiently large for each to generate a high level of business. ☐

   e) Are reachable in terms of communications. ☐

   f) Have relevance in regards to the purchasing decision. ☐

   g) Are not too many in number. ☐

   h) Provide a competitive advantage. ☐

   TOTAL (max. 80) ☐

3 Looking at the score in 2, is there any room for improvement regarding how your customers are segmented? *Note*: any total score much less than 80 is really unacceptable. Tick the appropriate boxes below.

a) Is the existing method of segmentation satisfactory?

YES ☐ NO ☐

b) Can the existing method be modified to make it more effective?

YES ☐ NO ☐

c) Must a new approach be devised for customer segmentation?

YES ☐ NO ☐

4 In the light of your response to 3, formulate your action plan regarding customer segmentation. *Note*: clearly, any new approach ought to score maximum marks in 2 above.

EXERCISE 2.2 CHOOSING A RESEARCH COMPANY

OBJECTIVE This shows how different research companies might be evaluated in order to arrive at the one most likely to meet your needs. Of course, not all of the factors shown are going to be equally relevant, that is why it could be important to introduce a system of weighting as shown below.

PROCEDURE Each competing research company is scored against each factor using a 1–5 scale.

1	2	3	4	5
Poor	Below average	Average	Above average	Very good

Each factor score can be multiplied by the weighting, which could be organised thus:

Very important	weighting of 3
Fairly important	weighting of 2
Useful	weighting of 1
Not applicable	weighting of 0

By following such a scoring process it is possible to add up the points for each column. The company achieving the highest score is clearly out-performing the others and is the one you should choose to conduct your research.

Points to Consider	Weighting	Company X	Company Y	Company Z
ORGANISATION AND RESOURCES				
1 Size				
2 Location (accessibility)				
3 No. full-time qualified staff				
4 No. part-time qualified staff				
5 Interview staff (permanent)				
6 Interview staff (part time)				
7 Type of qualifications and experience				
8 Extent of use of associations				
9 Terms of business				
10 Links with other companies or seats of learning				
11 Financial strengths/ soundness				
REPUTATION AND EXPERIENCE				
1 Reputation in general				

Points to Consider	Weighting	Company X	Company Y	Company Z
2 Reputation in area to be investigated 3 Reputation of individual members of staff 4 Extent of repeat business 5 Length of time in business 6 Degree of specialisation 7 Range of techniques available				
PROFESSIONALISM 1 Understanding of problem 2 Clarity of research design 3 Contribution of MR in general 4 Publications 5 Leadership of specific fields 6 Client recommendations				
TOTAL				

EXERCISE 2.3 COMPETITIVE ADVANTAGE CARD SORT

OBJECTIVE The objective of this exercise is to enable the process described in the chapter to be brought to life. It does not of course get down to mathematical calculations, but it does allow for experimentation and can provide some valuable insights about the company's competitive position in particular markets.

Another advantage of the 'card sort' approach is that, when used by a group, it can stimulate vital discussion about marketing subactivities and performance standards.

PROCEDURE

Preparation

At the back of this book are pages which need to be detached and cut up into 'cards' as instructed. There are two packs of cards to assemble:

PACK A   Which consists almost entirely of product or service features.

PACK B   Which consists mainly of relative performance standards, i.e., better, same or worse.

Having constructed the above packs of cards, these are the steps to follow:

STEP 1   Establish which product or service is going to be the focus for this exercise.

STEP 2   Take Pack A and on a table lay out the 'header' cards in this configuration:

Critical for success	Important	Fairly important	Useful	Not applicable

STEP 3   With the remainder of Pack A, the features cards, place them one at a time under the appropriate header card face upwards. In order that the cards can be read at all times they should be positioned in

columns, one under the other. Use the blank cards provided to make up any additional relevant features not covered by the printed pack. *Note*: It is not necessary for cards in the non-applicable column to be read and so these can be stacked and eventually discarded.

STEP 4   Having completed this initial sort, study the layout and reposition the cards until you are satisfied that they reflect the subject product or service in terms of its features/attributes. *Note*: If there are more than five cards in the 'critical for success' column, then it must be whittled down to five. (The reason for this is that only a small number of factors can be truly critical and it is important to be clear about what these are.)

STEP 5   With this initial card sort completed, look at the final layout as if it were the closing stages of a horse-race. The 'horses' are travelling from right to left and at the moment the 'critical cards' are in the lead. With this imagery in mind, ask yourself:

a) Are there any 'horses' that were making strong running but are now beginning to fall away?

b) Are there any 'horses' making a late surge and moving up through the field?

c) What are the reasons for these shifts?

Note: It will be useful to make a record of this overview and who the up and coming 'horses' are. This information can be used for comparison purposes at some future date.

STEP 6   Now just concentrate on the cards in the 'critical for success' column; the remainder can be put to one side. Arrange these five cards in a column so that the most important is at the top, the next most important below it and so on. As we saw in the chapter, the importance of each feature will relate to the level of benefits it brings to customers.

STEP 7   Take Pack B and arrange a new configuration of cards on the table using its 'header' cards, as shown:

		Competitor 1	Competitor 2	Competitor 3
Critical for	1	—	—	—
success	2	—	—	—
cards	3	—	—	—
	4	—	—	—
	5	—	—	—

Note: The lines represent where remaining cards will be positioned.

STEP 8   With actual competitors in mind for the competitor 'header' cards, consider critical success factor card 1. Depending upon how your company compares with the agreed competitors on this particular feature, place a 'better', 'same' or 'worse' card in position (top line row in illustration above).

STEP 9   Complete Step 8 for all remaining critical success cards. Study this final layout and make a note of it for future reference. Now consider what actions you can take to:

a) increase your competitive advantage where you are 'better' than your competitors;

b) establish a competitive advantage where you are the 'same';

c) Reduce the disadvantage where you are 'worse'.

STEP 10 Concentrating mainly on issues from the top portion of the layout (since these are the most important), calculate via cost vs benefits analysis the most productive action to take and formulate an improvement plan.

PACK A   Consists of the following cards:

Header cards

Critical for success   Ease of servicing
Important for success   Brand name

Fairly important for success
Useful for success
Not applicable for success

Technical competence
Quality
Performance
Design/style
Financial terms, e.g., discount
Finish
Colour
Installation/fitting provided
Versatility/flexibility
Trade-in value
Size (product)
Price
Packaging
Delivery (on time)
Method of shipment
Life expectancy
Maintenance costs
Running costs

Company reputation
Product/service image
Exclusivity
Administrative efficiency
Production strengths
Size of operations
Environmentally friendly
Patents/copyright
Safety features
Ease of use
Training provided
Compatible extras
Distribution network
Approval, e.g., BSI
Availability
Weight
Novelty value
After-sales servicing
Promotion
Quality of workforce
Guarantees/warranties

PACK B   This pack consists of:
One card marked   Competitor 1
One card marked   Competitor 2
One card marked   Competitor 3

Fifteen cards marked   Better
Fifteen cards marked   Same
Fifteen cards marked   Worse

3 Benchmarking the feel good factor

In Chapter 2 it was shown what could be done to ensure that the basic product or service was competitive. Now it is necessary to consider how to enhance the feel good factor that customers experience from their transactions with the company.

However, first of all it is important to be clear about the term 'benchmarking', for it is a word that is creeping into the management vocabulary with increasing frequency. Put simply it is a means of searching for the best practices that will lead to outstanding company performance. By aiming for nothing short of the best possible industrial or commercial practices, the organisation is forced to face up to the harsh realities of what really needs to be tackled in order to outscore its competitors.

The benchmarking process merely provides a means for the company to compare its own practices with those which are perceived as being excellent. This process can be applied to products, services or even manufacturing processes and provides not only a means of measurement, but also a basis for target-setting for improvement. Useful though this approach can be, it would be naive to believe that it can provide all the answers and solve every problem at a stroke. Instead, it is more than likely that it will cause a high degree of consternation in some quarters of the company, as long-held 'folk wisdom' is shown up as lacking true substance. Moreover, it is equally possible that some management 'sacred cows' will have to lose their cherished status and take their chances in the new secular culture where hard data outweighs opinion.

In this chapter there will be a brief look at the origins of benchmarking, the process steps which need to be covered and its particular application to improving the feel good component of customer service.

ORIGINS

It is widely accepted that benchmarking was developed by the Xerox Corporation in the USA during the late 1970s and early 1980s. Initially the process was used to examine the manufacturing costs of selected products. The operating performance and product features of competing copying machines were compared, together with a critical analysis of their construction, manufacturing processes and component parts.

The company found to its horror that some competing machines (mainly Japanese) could be sold for less than it took Xerox to make them. This analysis forced the company to adopt benchmarks used by their competitors and to work to radically new standards which were hitherto beyond their 'mind-set'. Such was the success of this approach that it was gradually refined and applied to other areas of the business. The rest, as they say, is history.

THE BASIC BENCHMARKING PROCESS

The basic process is shown in Figure 3.1. As it illustrates, a series of steps have to be accomplished in order to extract the full benefits of benchmarking. If any of these individual steps are missed out or short-changed in some way then the whole process becomes fatally flawed. It is therefore important at the outset that we are clear about what is involved at each of the steps on the benchmarking 'staircase'.

Step 1   Identifying the subject area

Because the benchmarking technique can be applied to virtually any aspect of the business, it is necessary to think about which particular focal point should be the subject of attention. Clearly, the ultimate choice should be an area which is critical to the company's future success and as a result yields the prospect of a high 'payback'.

Generally speaking it is the outputs of the organisation which have the greatest impact on its competitive position; thus products

Figure 3.1 The benchmarking 'staircase'

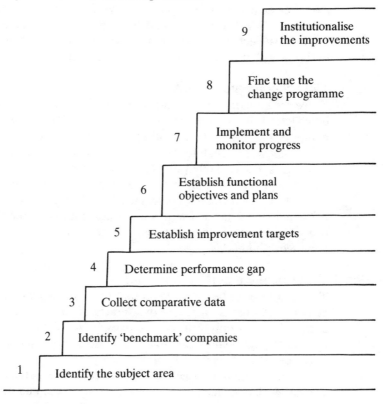

9 — Institutionalise the improvements

8 — Fine tune the change programme

7 — Implement and monitor progress

6 — Establish functional objectives and plans

5 — Establish improvement targets

4 — Determine performance gap

3 — Collect comparative data

2 — Identify 'benchmark' companies

1 — Identify the subject area

and services can be particularly fertile subject areas. Equally the activities which go into the product surround, such as service, shipment, order processing and so on, can be valuable topics to put under the microscope, since they also constitute organisational outputs.

Step 2   Identify 'benchmark' companies

Having identified the subject area, it becomes possible to begin to identify the organisations against whom it is meaningful to make comparisons. Those which immediately spring to mind are likely to be main competitors, or the market leaders in one's particular sphere of business.

While it is right to select some companies which fall into these categories, it is not enough to rely solely on comparisons with them alone. Benchmarking sets out to strive for excellence, therefore companies which are renowned for superior performance in the relevant subject area, even if they are not in the same line of business, will also need to figure in the comparative framework.

Step 3 Collect comparative data

There are no hard and fast rules regarding the way the data should be collected, because the subject area will obviously influence the nature of the information required and the best ways of collecting it. For now it is enough to recognise that a vast array of researching techniques are available (as mentioned in Chapter 2), to be used either singly or in combination. Selecting the most appropriate methods can be a creative challenge for the benchmarker. That this particular step is tackled well is of paramount importance because everything which follows is based on the comparative data which are uncovered at this stage.

Step 4 Determine the performance gap

The data have to be analysed so that the company's performance can be evaluated against the practices of the benchmark companies. Not only will the company be required to identify its relative strengths and weaknesses, but also to understand why it is either better or worse and by how much.

It is at this analysis stage that one can capitalise on the quality of the earlier data collection. The more objective the measures used, the more accurately the performance gap can be defined. There is, however, another consideration to take into account regarding how the gap might be construed, and this takes into account the overriding dynamic perspective; that is to say, the relative rate of improvement and developments in the subject area. For example, supposing a company needed three years to bridge its current gap with the benchmark standards. If everybody moved on and developed their operating practices in the meantime (as they surely would), then three years hence the company could easily find itself just as far adrift from excellence as it is today.

Step 5 Establish improvement targets

Taking into account where performance is today and where it needs to be in the future enables improvement targets to be set.

Step 6 Establish functional objectives and plans

The nettle of change ultimately has to be grasped by the various functional departments which have a part to play in the improvement scenario. It invariably helps to gain commitment to the changes if the departments in question are involved in the planning process. In this way those who will actually have to make the future 'come alive' can bring to the change process all of their relevant experience and technical skills.

Step 7 Implement plans and monitor progress

The time for planning comes to an end and all the preparation is converted into action. Progress should be monitored in order to check that improvements are proceeding in an orderly way. Also, the background to the subject area should be monitored so that any sea changes in operating practices brought about by, for instance, a new application of computer technology, can be picked up.

Step 8 Fine-tune the change programme

From time to time the monitoring process will indicate that the pace of change is losing momentum, or that day-to-day problems are deflecting the initiative from its original target. In these circumstances some corrective fine-tuning will be required to get everything back on track.

Step 9 Institutionalise the improvements

As benefits begin to appear from the unfolding of the benchmarking process they should be woven into the fabric of the organisation. So, for example, if new individual performance standards become established in a particular activity, then these standards should be seen to drive the recruitment, rewards and promotion processes that prevail. Similarly, if improvements in administration were identified, then all earlier procedures should be downgraded or discredited.

In this way the general thrust and energy developed by the improvement process is harnessed into organisational life as something central and important, not as a 'Johnnie come lately' peripheral activity on the fringes.

As with any illustration in a book, the benchmarking process can look deceptively simple in outline. Yet, because it is a continuous process of measuring against the best, in reality it requires the highest level of commitment from top management and staff alike. Success will only be achieved by hard work and application. Such is the pervasive quality of benchmarking that it has the power to challenge the existing corporate culture in the ongoing search for excellence. While in itself this might be no bad thing, it is quite conceivable that the less progressive spirits in the organisation will fight a covert rearguard action to maintain something of the status quo. Organisational behaviour can sometimes be rather like the equation from Newtonian physics which asserts that for every action there is an equal and opposite reaction. Thus resistance to change can be expected at various levels, and only underpins the fact that management must pursue benchmarking with a whole-hearted determination if they are to harvest the true fruits of their labour.

It must also be remembered that logical and analytical though the process is, it is still subservient to the professional judgement of those who use it. In this sense benchmarking is a servant of top management, not its master. As a technique for delivering organis-ational improvement its effectiveness is therefore largely depen-dent upon the skill, ingenuity and tenacity of its users.

THE PROCESS APPLIED TO DEVELOPING THE FEEL GOOD FACTOR

Step 1   Clarifying the subject area

Having pinpointed the feel good factor as the subject area it now becomes important to establish exactly what components contri-bute to it in a particular business. A sample list of what these might be is given in Figure 3.2.

Before proceeding further it will be useful to have some idea about the relative importance of these various components. One straightforward way of doing this is to ask a representative sample of customers to rank them in order of importance, with the most important being ranked '1', the second '2' and so on. By averaging out such customer rankings it is possible to make a fairly accurate assessment of how they perceive 'customer service'.

Another method which could be used would be to combine a scoring system with a weighting factor for each component of service. Yet another approach would be to invite the sample of

Figure 3.2 Components of customer service that contribute to the feel
good factor (example)

Availability of items

After-sales service and backup

Efficient paperwork ordering system

Efficient telephone handling of orders and queries

Reliability of deliveries

Availability of published materials

Guarantee conditions

Order cycle time

Quality of face-to-face contacts

---

customers to distribute 100 points between the component factors
in such a way as to indicate their relative importance.

As with any use made of customer sampling, it is vitally
important that the samples themselves are truly representative of
the target population. It is also essential to determine if the sample
should represent just one or two specific market segments, or
customers as a whole. This is because, at a later stage, it might
become apparent that it is necessary to develop different customer
service 'packages' for different market segments. The wrong choice
of samples would deny this valuable information the opportunity
to surface.

Step 2 Establish the benchmarks

By referring to the list of feel good components given in Figure 3.2
and considering both some competing companies and paragons of
excellence in other types of business it becomes possible to establish the target benchmarks of performance at which to aim. It goes
without saying that these have to be as specific as possible,
although some qualitative judgements inevitably creep into consideration.

Thus, for example:

1   Availability of items could be measured in percentage of times

available, or the converse, percentage out of stock situations.

2   After-sales service and backup, by call-out times, complaint percentages, etc.

3   Efficient paperwork ordering system, by number of errors or customer complaints.

4   Efficient telephone ordering and handling of queries, by connection times, accuracy and 'friendliness'.

5   Reliability of deliveries, by plus or minus promised time.

6   Availability of published materials, per item.

7   Guarantee conditions, by number or generosity of conditions.

8   Order cycle time, by time from receipt to delivery.

9   Quality of face-to-face contacts by number of complaints, or customer sampling targets.

By examining as much hard data as possible it becomes feasible to identify the benchmarks in each area which represent high, if not excellent, standards of performance. Equally, by looking at a range of competitors and also some excellent companies, it becomes possible to assess the spread of service in terms of what levels

Figure 3.3 Examples of sources of benchmarking information

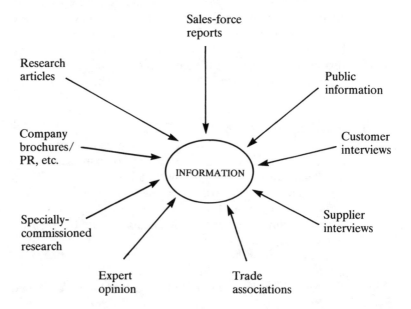

constitute the worst and the best. Also, it must be borne in mind that even the best can fall short of customers' expectations.

The way this information is obtained will reflect on the resourcefulness of the person responsible for benchmarking and also the physical resources made available to him or her. Some of the sources of information are shown in Figure 3.3.

Step 3 Collecting comparative data

Whereas collecting benchmarking information is essentially externally directed, many of the company's measures of performance will be available internally from sales records and the like. Although some external information might be required to supplement that which is available in the company, the overall task is, on the whole, significantly easier.

Step 4 Determine the performance gap

It now becomes possible to put the data collected to constructive use, as shown in Figure 3.4. It can be seen that the various factors which contribute to customer satisfaction are now listed in order of importance as rated *by customers*. The plotting of performance levels in the way shown in Figure 3.4 provides an easily-grasped visual presentation of the performance gap.

Step 5 Establish improvement targets

From Figure 3.4 it can be seen that the prime areas of improvement should be those areas which are of high concern to customers and where our performance falls short of the benchmark.

Of immediate significance is the 'availability of items'. Not only is this the prime concern of customers, but it is also the area of our biggest shortfall against the benchmark.

Looking at the other elements of customer service, in terms of their customer ranking, we can see that order cycle time is not bettered by anyone, whereas 'reliability of deliveries' falls short of the benchmark. Similarly, when it comes to 'face-to-face contacts' our quality is found wanting. Another area where the company falls down is that of 'handling telephone orders and queries'. Here there is quite a wide performance gap. On the 'ordering system', 'after-sales service' and 'guarantees' the company is second to none, but again it fails to excel in the 'availability of published materials'.

Figure 3.4 Example of a customer service benchmarking profile

Components of the feel good factor	Customer ranking	Performance level Poor 1 2 3 Excellent 4 5
Availability of items	1	
Order cycle time	2	
Reliability of deliveries	3	
Quality of contacts	4	
Efficient handling of phone and queries	5	
Efficient ordering system	6	
After-sales service and backup	7	
Guarantee conditions	8	
Availability of published materials	9	

Notes: ○-----○ Our performance

✗———✗ Benchmark performance

Although 5 = excellent on the scale, the highest benchmark is only plotted at 4, to accommodate times when the company measure might be higher.

From this type of analysis clear clues can be obtained about *where* there is a need for improvement, and, more importantly, the standards which it is necessary to achieve. Thus, in the example shown in Figure 3.4 the improvement areas are:

1   Improve availability of items.
2   Improve reliability of deliveries.
3   Improve quality of face-to-face contacts.
4   Improve telephone handling of orders and queries.
5   Improve the availability of published materials.

Of these 'availability' is clearly the main issue to address. However, 'quality contacts' and 'telephone handling' might be next in importance because of the large performance gap. 'Published materials' is obviously not in the same league as far as priorities go.

Step 6 Establish functional objectives and plans

If, for the purposes of providing an example, we concentrate just on the issue of improving the availability of products to the benchmark standard, we need to delve a little deeper into the situation. By analysing the reasons for the past substandard performance, it becomes possible to identify specific functional objectives. Again, the method for doing this will be a matter of personal choice, but one useful approach is the 'why–why?' diagram (see Figure 3.5).

Figure 3.5 Example of how the 'why–why?' diagram can be developed to identify the functional roots of the problem

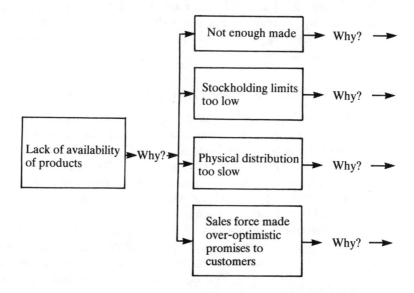

As we can see in the example provided by Figure 3.5 the 'asking why?' process discloses a number of possible reasons for the non-availability of product. In the diagram the various threads are not taken to their conclusion, essential though that would be in real life. For now it is enough to see that the resolution of the 'availability' problem could result in functional objectives and plans being set for at least:

> The production department
> The warehousing/dispatch department
> The sales department.

The nature of these objectives and plans themselves would to a large extent depend upon where the various strands of the 'why–why?' diagram reached their conclusion. Thus, for example, the manufacturing objectives could conceivably be to secure better supplies of raw materials, to reduce scrap or remove bottlenecks in production. The analytical approach shown here would enable the company to establish which of these would be the most pertinent objectives to attain the benchmark so critical for future success.

Steps 7, 8 and 9 Implementing, fine-tuning and institutionalising

Enough has been said earlier about these final steps on the bench-marking staircase to make it redundant to add anything further. However, there is perhaps one additional issue which ought to be addressed.

RECALIBRATING THE BENCHMARKS

Because benchmarking is a dynamic process which takes place against an ever-restless and volatile background of a particular industry or sphere of business, it would be naive to imagine that once set benchmarks last for ever. The multi-talented and resourceful Phileas Fogg struggled to achieve the benchmark of going around the world in eighty days. Today an equivalent target would be measured in hours.

Therefore, as a matter of routine, say about once a year, the benchmarks chosen should be re-examined and if necessary re-calibrated. Although some will complain and mutter guardedly about moving the goalposts, it must be remembered that progress obeys no rules ... except to move on.

SUMMARY

In this chapter the technique of benchmarking has been intro-duced. It is a process which involves nine sequential steps, and its objective is to enable a company to compare itself in chosen areas against current best practice. The practitioners of the said best practice might be within the company's own industry, or be operating in some other field.

We showed how the technique could be used specifically to improve the feel good factor. However, the benchmarking process has to be fuelled with accurate information, much of which can only be gleaned from research, if it is to be of genuine value. Although the original thrust for benchmarking customer service might come from a marketer, the process can lead to corrective actions being taken in all corners of the organisation.

Like some other management techniques, benchmarking is an aid to decision-making and organisational improvement. Yet, analytical though the process is, it is still subservient to the professional judgement of those who use it. Also, it is an exercise which, once started, needs to be repeated on a regular basis. This is because new technology or creative thinking can lead to current benchmarks becoming superseded by newer, more appropriate ones.

EXERCISE 3.1 WHAT IS THE FEEL GOOD PACKAGE?

OBJECTIVE In the context of your particular business what components of organisational activity serve to make your customers feel good, i.e., not the actual product or service itself?

PROCEDURE Make a list below:

> When the list is completed to your satisfaction, run down it again writing 'F' against each item where there is factual evidence that customers value this, and 'O' where this is based on opinion.

EXERCISE 3.2 PRIORITISATION

PROCEDURE

1 Taking the list generated in Exercise 3.1 identify and rank the ten components that contribute most to the feel good factor as seen by customers, so that 1 is the most important, 2 the next and so on. *Note*: it is worth getting the views of some work colleagues at this stage so that the end result reflects a consensus view, rather than that of an individual (which might be unintentionally biased).

Record these components below:

Ranking   1
           2
           3
           4
           5
           6
           7
           8
           9
          10

2 Although the above are reckoned to be the ten most important components which contribute to the feel good factor, is this list based on items of fact or opinion? (Check back at the list in Exercise 3.1 and look for the 'F's and the 'O's). If a significant number of 'O's appear in the

prioritised list, then clearly too much is being based on opinions and therefore some market research data would be very helpful. It could be counter-productive to proceed with the benchmarking technique if the factors under consideration are not really the key issues from the customers' viewpoint.

EXERCISE 3.3 BENCHMARKING THE FEEL GOOD FACTOR

PROCEDURE Using the prioritised list developed from Exercises 3.1 and 3.2, and having verified that this accurately reflects what customers' perceive as making them feel good (by using research where necessary), complete the benchmarking process. This will entail:

1 Quantifying how these factors will be measured.
2 Identifying benchmark companies.
3 Collecting comparative data.
4 Establishing the performance gap.
5 Setting improvement targets.
6 Translating these into functional objectives and plans.
7 Monitoring progress.
8 Fine-tuning the improvement process.
9 Institutionalising the improvements into working practices, systems, etc.

All of these steps are described in this chapter.

4 *Quality can't be left to chance*

In the two previous chapters the concepts of getting the basic product or service right and developing the feel good factor were based entirely on what the customer values. In this sense, what the customer perceives as quality is quality. Indeed, this is customer orientation being applied in real terms. Taking this line of thought further, it follows that if quality is defined in terms of customer expectations, then where there is a shortfall on the part of the company, it is perceived as a quality gap by the customer.

Logical though this might be, it does present some problems regarding the setting of quality standards. It is easy to see why. Let us put ourselves in the customer's shoes for a moment and imagine that we are interested in learning to drive. Suppose the choice before us is to enrol for lessons with either a large company which operates on a national basis and advertises on television, or a local one-man band. Whatever our choice, if something went wrong would we perceive the quality gap in the same way? The chances are that we would, in all probability, be far more tolerant of the shortcomings in the service provided by the local instructor. This is because our expectations would be coloured by the nature of the supplier himself and the obviously limited scale of his resources. We would not expect him to match the large company in everything. Thus the quality gap can be seen as a product of the facts of the situation and judgements about the surrounding circumstances, since it is both of these factors which influence the customers' perceptions.

Clearly, defining quality in customer terms and understanding the quality gap is not quite as simple as it might at first appear to be. Studies have shown that there are four potential reasons why quality gaps occur:

1 Managers do not know what customers expect.
2 There is no management commitment to provide what customers expect.
3 There is variable performance in meeting customer expectations.
4 Customer expectations are enhanced by promotional communications and the subsequent offering does not live up to these.

These possible reasons for misunderstandings can make impact either individually or in combination.

It is the task of those managing customer service to ensure that quality gaps, from whatever origins, are minimised if not eliminated. Therefore, like it or not, providing customer service in the final analysis boils down to providing quality. This point has been grasped by the more forward-looking companies who have aligned their service quality strategies with the concept of total quality management (TQM).

TQM

Total quality management is an organisation-wide approach which seeks to improve performance, that is to say quality service delivery, on a continuous and systematic basis. The thrust of TQM programmes is to satisfy the requirements of all customers through the development of error-free processes within the organisation.

The origins of TQM go back to the 1950s and the work of the two management science gurus, Deming and Juran. Although their message for quality fell on deaf ears in their homeland, the USA, it struck a resonant chord in Japan. The consequence of this can be seen by studying the numerous articles and case-studies that have been written about the rise of Japanese industry and its subsequent dominance of world markets in so many types of businesses, for example, cameras, motor cycles, zip fasteners, shipbuilding, keyboard instruments, etc. At the heart of this success was the fact that quality was being built into these products due to the dedication of all those involved in supplying them.

Apologists for inferior western products failed to recognise this success for what it was, but instead talked about different cultures and management practices which would not work or be acceptable elsewhere. Of course, this myth has now been exploded, but it took until the early 1980s for the underlying philosophy of quality management to take root in the UK.

Of course, that pithy Yorkshire adage that one gets 'owt for nowt' is perfectly true. There is a cost involved in striving to introduce TQM, but at the same time there is a hidden cost associated with not introducing some form of quality management. It has been estimated that something between 25 and 40 per cent of all effort expended in British industry and commerce is spent on correcting problems which originate in one part of the organisation and have negative knock-on efforts elsewhere internally or, worse still, with external customers. Thus there is a rich reward awaiting those organisations who get things right first time every time.

Those companies who have adopted a TQM approach find that they benefit in a number of ways:

1   The organisational focus being firmly on the customer means that internecine rivalry inside the company is reduced and resources are better allocated.
2   More people within the organisation take a responsibility for quality and take action when it is required.
3   Team working is encouraged.
4   Time wasting and error-ridden procedures are eliminated.
5   Better procedures are developed.
6   Performance is better understood and can be measured on a consistent basis.
7   The dangers of complacency are reduced by the restless quest for improved quality customer service.

In more concrete terms, what emerge are stories about significant savings or improvements in market standing which can be directly attributable to this new approach.

TQM can be seen as the hub around which four interrelated activities revolve, as in Figure 4.1. We will look at each of these activities in turn.

1 Documenting the quality management system

The starting-point for TQM is to document the way the company sets about maintaining the quality of its products and services throughout their manufacture and delivery. The purpose of doing

Figure 4.1 The TQM approach in outline

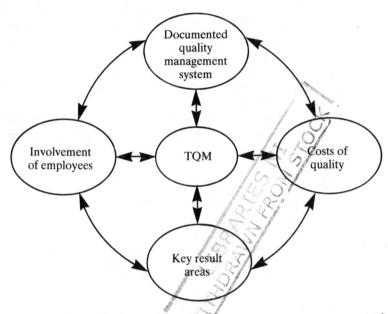

this is to ensure that promises made to a customer at a contract stage are delivered on a consistent basis. In the UK there has been a move to develop quality standards through certification association with the British Standards Institute's BS5750. (This was developed in post-war years to ensure that suppliers to NATO produced goods of consistent quality. Its international equivalent is ISO9000.)[1] By meeting these externally imposed standards, the supplier's capabilities are thereby not only endorsed but given an added credibility. Such is the acceptance of this measure of company 'fitness' that many customers will now only contemplate doing business with suppliers who are accredited.

In order to become registered in the UK, a company has to determine its quality system standards which are then independently audited by approved assessors in terms of meeting the standards set by BS5750. Moreover, the auditing process will ensure that those in the organisation responsible for operating the

[1] The particular Quality Assurance Specification which relates to Marketing, Sales and Customer Assurance is BS5750 Part 1: 1987. Its European and international equivalents are EN29001 and ISO9001 respectively.

various quality procedures do in fact follow them. Rigorous though this examination is, the number of companies registering with the BSI continues to rise every year. It is also interesting to note that whereas the initial enthusiasm for this scheme came from manufacturing industry, more recently service companies have shown an equal willingness to respond. It is not unusual to find businesses as diverse as financial services, training consultancies and street-cleaning being registered.

This initial step of documentation can be a daunting task for the badly-organised company and is perhaps one of the major hurdles to be overcome. It is necessary to go through all operating procedures and collect them into a quality manual which will contain all documentation and standard instructions. Indeed, it becomes the organisational 'bible', explaining as it does the corporate policy with regard to quality. Some of the issues it might include could be:

1 The mission statement regarding quality.
2 The organisational structure for quality.
3 The senior manager responsible overall.
4 Responsibility of others.
5 The overriding principles behind all operating systems.
6 How and when procedures will be audited internally.
7 Functional procedures, for example, for production these might include purchases and inventory control, tracing work in progress, process control, product safety, testing and measuring equipment, finishing processes and standards, packaging and so on. (See Figure 4.2 which provides an example.)

From such a brief explanation it can be seen that not only must the quality manual be comprehensive, but also it becomes a unique document for the organisation. It is not something that can be bought off the shelf, nor, for that matter, is it something that an outside consultant can easily draw up – although they can, at times, make useful contributions.

By now it should be unnecessary to stress this point, but we will: the procedures which go into the quality manual should always take into account the requirements of customers, since they should be the arbiters of all quality standards. Customer expectations should be at the heart of all management operations, whether the

Figure 4.2 An example of part of a quality manual (training consultancy)

■ COMPLAINTS PROCEDURE

(*Note:* complaints are extremely rare, but when they occur this procedure must be followed.)

*   If a complaint is made the consultant seeks to deal with and put it right at initial level. Such complaints are reported to the director, together with the official outcome of the consultant's intervention.

*   If it is a more difficult complaint to resolve the director will become involved.

*   If the complaint is not resolved at this level, it will then be fully investigated and appropriate remedial action carried out in accordance with the terms of reference incorporated in the submission upon which the assignment was agreed.

*   In extreme cases this may involve either a reduction in the client fee or cancellation of the fee entirely.

*   There is recourse to the chairman if required, but it has never been necessary to draw on this.

*   The company has a detailed set of legal procedures for dealing with customer complaints which is laid down in its contracts document – Standard Conditions of Offer and Contract for Research and Consultancy (*Appendix VI*).

All client complaints are treated very seriously and if, after all investigation, weaknesses in our approach or procedures come to light, then the chairman and director will bring this to the attention of the consultant meeting, where measures to avoid recurrence will be agreed and procedures to implement such measures instigated.

issue is about developing new products or services or how the switchboard should be manned. Failure to recognise this is more far-reaching than being turned down by the quality auditors.

2 The costs of quality

Just as a mariner would, quite literally, be all at sea without a compass to guide him, so managers would be equally perplexed to know which way to turn without having some notion about the costs of their actions. Quality costing has two components:

1   Open costs: these are the more obvious areas of cost such as handling customer complaints, recalling faulty goods and replacing them, scrap and reworking, honouring warranties and the like.
2   Hidden costs: These are mainly intangible and reflect the input which goes into products and services to ensure that they are right first time.

Another way of looking at this cost formula is shown in Figure 4.3. From this it can be recognised that whereas the costs of failure are out and out losses, the prevention costs could be seen as an investment which should eventually lead to failure costs reducing over time. If this is true, as many experts claim, then as quality improves the cost of quality actually decreases.

Figure 4.3 The quality cost equation

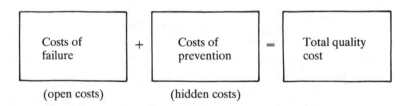

| | Costs of failure | | Costs of prevention | | Total quality cost |
| (open costs) | | | (hidden costs) | | |

The intangible nature of the hidden prevention costs means that often, at best, they can only be estimated. However, in most companies knowing the costs of failure (and the reasons for incurring them) can present managers with incentive enough to take action.

Figure 4.4 The improvement area matrix

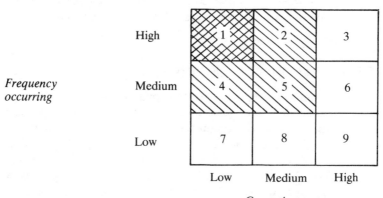

Frequency occurring

High

Medium

Low

Low   Medium   High

Correction costs

Key: ⊠ main impact area, ◩ next best

3 Identify the key result areas

Faced with a range of possible actions to improve quality it is essential that energy and resources are invested in those areas with the prospect of greatest success. After all, every reduction in quality costs effectively increases revenue without the need for selling any extra units.

Managers will have their favourite methods of identifying the areas to be tackled. Invariably somewhere in their reasoning will be the application of the 80/20 law. Thus 80 per cent of the total quality costs will be attributable to 20 per cent of the possible causes. This might be a useful starting-point. Similarly, 80 per cent of the complaints will be addressed to 20 per cent of the possible reasons for complaint. It is possible to combine these two pieces of information in the matrix shown in Figure 4.4, which helps to identify improvement areas.

By considering one product or service at a time, it should be possible to plot most of the quality cost areas on a matrix of this type. From the resulting pattern it becomes clear that the cost factors which appear in box 1 are the simplest to tackle since they cost little to correct but crop up frequently (thereby using up valuable resources). Using similar reasoning, the three areas adjacent to this box (boxes 2, 4 and 5) might be equally fruitful. If it came to making a choice between alternatives that appear in these boxes, then 'value to the customer' should be one criterion to consider.

4 Involvement of employees

It is self-evident that no scheme of TQM will succeed without the involvement of employees. Most of the next chapter addresses this issue.

THE NEED FOR A CO-ORDINATOR

From the foregoing text it is apparent that in most companies it is no small task to get a total quality management approach up and running and to administer BS5750 or its equivalent. It is hardly possible for a manager to take this on as a spare-time activity whenever his 'real' job gives him brief moments of opportunity. For this reason many companies create the post of a quality manager whose task is to plan and manage the completion of all the activities relevant to TQM.

It must be emphasised that the quality manager achieves success by orchestrating the organisational efforts. Thus he or she is a blend of facilitator, internal consultant, change strategist, trainer, coach and counsellor rolled up into one. The most common problem that distracts many quality managers and reduces their effectiveness is that they are seen as a scapegoat for everything that goes wrong. Of course, it is a convenient strategy for lazy operations managers to try to shuffle off their responsibility for quality on to the quality manager, but to do so is missing the whole point of total quality management and acts to the detriment of the organisation at large.

MAINTAINING A CUSTOMER FOCUS

Because customers are the final arbiters of quality, it is essential for the company to maintain some sort of dialogue with them and to *listen* to what they say. There are a number of ways of achieving this, providing there is the organisational willingness to do so.

Analysing customer complaints

This is one obvious way of gathering information about customer expectations, although in this case it has more to do with how they were not met. However, it must be remembered that for every customer who is dissatisfied and complains, there are many more who are equally dissatisfied yet, for reasons best known to them-

Figure 4.5 The complaints iceberg

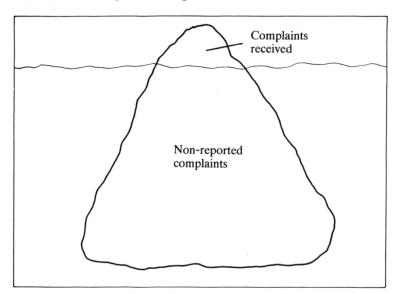

Complaints
received

Non-reported
complaints

selves, say nothing. Thus customer complaints should be seen as something of an iceberg as shown in Figure 4.5. The visible tip, revealed by complaints, does little to convey the mass which lies below the surface. With an iceberg it is estimated that about seven-eighths is invisible. What might it be for complaints?

Because complainants are in the minority, their views might be skewed in some way. For example, they might represent the higher educated end of the market, or a specific socio-economic group. There is likely to be something about them which gives them the confidence and determination to complain when others remain silent. It is to the company's advantage to be aware of the ways in which this valuable feedback might be distorted before acting on it in any large-scale manner.

Of course, all individual complaints must be handled speedily, efficiently and courteously. If the complaint cannot be dealt with quickly, then it is good practice to get back to the customer promptly and to acknowledge that the matter is in hand.

A systematic analysis of complaints in terms of their nature, frequency, origins, costs to rectify and so on will provide a valuable input for improving quality.

Analysing compliments

Some companies might find themselves in the fortunate position of being able to do this, but on the whole even the most satisfied and best-intentioned of customers rarely get round to conveying their approval. When they do arrive, the occasional endorsements can be valuable morale boosters to staff. They can also be used for public relations purposes, providing proof that the company's claims of service and quality are not hollow promises.

Questionnaires

Getting customers to complete questionnaires is a common and relatively inexpensive way of collecting information. This can be accomplished in a number of ways, for example, as an enclosure with a product, at the point of contact, for example, an hotel room, sending it through the post, in connection with responses to advertisements or special offers and so on.

The success rate in getting a response from a questionnaire can be highly variable since it is dependent on a number of contingent factors. Important among these are:

1   the design of the questionnaire;
2   the selection of the sample; and
3   the degree of incentives provided.

1 Design of the questionnaire

There is more to designing a questionnaire than meets the eye. There are a number of ground rules to follow in order to avoid the common pitfalls that beset the inexperienced. These are:

1   Explain the purpose for seeking the information and how it is going to be used.
2   Keep the layout simple.
3   Keep the questions short and unambiguous and avoid leading questions.
4   Let there be a logical sequence to its overall design.
5   Ask easy, less personal questions at the beginning and only move gradually to a more difficult or sensitive area.
6   Make it easy to return.
7   Thank the person for their co-operation.
8   Ensure that answers can be coded to assist analysis.

Figure 4.6 An example of an hotel type of questionnaire

1   If you've not stayed with us before from what source did
    you learn about this hotel?

    Magazine   ☐

    AA/RAC guide   ☐

    Word of mouth   ☐

    Newspaper advert ☐

2   Was your booking processed quickly and efficiently?
    Yes / No

3   Were the Reception staff friendly and helpful?
    Yes / No

4   Was your room clean and tidy?
    Yes / No

5   If you have eaten in the restaurant was the food well
    prepared and presented?
    Yes / No

6   Were the waiters/waitresses friendly and welcoming?
    Yes / No

7   If you have used Room Service was your request
    handled punctually and efficiently?
    Yes / No

8   Do you have any recommendations that would help us
    make your stay more enjoyable?
    Yes / No
    If Yes, please outline your suggestion below:
    ....
    ....
    ....
    ....
    ....
    ....

9   Explain the purpose for seeking the information and how it is going to be used.

The first point is particularly important and has been found to have considerable bearing on the respondents' attitudes regarding the care and attention that is paid to the questionnaire.

There are additional considerations to take into account regarding a questionnaire, such as offering multiple choices, ticked boxes, having spaces for additional comments and the like. However, often the depth of information required and the nature of the target audience will determine which approach is likely to be the most appropriate. Figure 4.6 is an example of the type of questionnaire often found in hotel rooms.

2 Selection of the sample
There are two issues which need to be addressed regarding the selection of customer samples. One is concerned with the size of the sample, the other with its homogeneity.

Sample size can be calculated roughly by referring to Table 4.1. It can be seen that the sample size reduces considerably (as a proportion of the population) as the target population increases. Hence relatively small samples can still manage to provide meaningful information for huge populations. However, to be strictly accurate the figures in Table 4.1 refer to populations which have a consistency about them. Therefore for companies that have segmented their customers into distinctive groups, the above sampling figures would hold reasonably true within each segment. In contrast, if the customer population was ill-defined or quite arbitrary then the table figures would have to be used with great caution, and, without a doubt, sample sizes would need to be much larger.

Table 4.1 Population and sample size

Population	100	250	500	1,000	2,000	4,000	10,000	20,000
Sample		80	145	210	285	335	360	365	370

3 Providing incentives

The response rate from questionnaires can be increased dramatically by providing an element of incentive for their return. This is particularly true for lengthy and in-depth questionnaires. Exactly how this is done and the nature of the incentive will depend on the circumstances. So, for example, information might be received accompanying a guarantee registration, alternatively, respondents might be entered in a free draw, given vouchers, a special offer, a free sample or a small gift. There is considerable scope for creativity regarding what form the incentive might take.

Telephone surveys

This can be a quick method to generate information and does enable the 'researcher' to seek clarification to ambiguous responses from customers. It also carries with it an element of PR. However, it also has some drawbacks in that the call needs to be kept short and to the point. Moreover, some people do not like their privacy being invaded in this way and if the timing is inconvenient (say the person is eating or watching a favourite television programme) not much thought will be given to the responses.

Customer groups and user panels

These consist ideally of 'typical' groups of customers who can be led in discussion among themselves, or in a group with the company's staff, about issues which are of mutual concern. Such a process can provide valuable insights, but at the same time it is too often a case of getting willing panel members rather than typical ones. This means that the feedback received might not be truly representative. Also, depending upon how the situation is managed, the customers might see their role to be ultra-critical or, worse still, be too embarrassed to voice their real concerns.

Use outside researchers

There was reference to this in Chapter 2 (p. 26) and there is little point in elaborating further.

Other methods

There are a number of other methods which can be tried, such as freephone responses, video points, mystery shoppers and the like. Like all other approaches they each have some merits and demerits.

LISTEN TO THOSE INSIDE THE ORGANISATION

Quite rightly, the company must spend much of its time listening to customers. However, it would be equally well served to listen to its own staff from time to time. Although many might seem like spectators on the sidelines of some sporting event, they do nevertheless see occasional patterns of play of which even the main participants are unaware. The views of the company's management and staff can be elicited in a number of different ways, including:

- Attitude surveys
- Suggestion schemes
- Competitions
- Conferences and workshops.

The most suitable vehicle for tapping internal views will be very much dependent upon the size of the company and what is acceptable to its particular culture.

SUMMARY

We have seen that quality standards, whether they relate to the basic product or service or the feel good factor, must be based on what customers perceive as quality. However, this seemingly obvious statement is complicated because customers' expectations of quality are coloured by subjective judgements about the surrounding circumstances. For example, expectations for a meal at a four-star hotel and a transport cafe would be vastly different because they would be influenced by the resources available to each supplier.

Quality gaps occur because managers do not know what customers expect, they are not committed to providing what customers expect, there is variable performance in meeting customer expectations or because customer expectations are enhanced by promotional hyperbole, against which the subsequent offer falls short.

Forward-looking companies have tried to overcome the quality gap by aligning their customer service to the concept of total quality management (TQM). This involves documenting the way quality is managed throughout the company, knowing much more about the costs of quality (both open and hidden), identifying the key result areas and adopting a high level of employee involvement.

The introduction of TQM is no easy task, for in addition to the administration required, the organisation must maintain a customer focus to ensure that its quality standards are up to date. A number of different methods for obtaining customer feedback were discussed. Implicit in approaches like TQM is that, in addition to listening to customers, the organisation also listens, more attentively, to its own staff, for they can be the source of many competition-beating ideas.

EXERCISE 4.1 MEASURING THE QUALITY GAP

OBJECTIVE This exercise can be applied to any product or service. It can also be used to prompt discussion in small groups.

PROCEDURE
PRODUCT/SERVICE UNDER REVIEW ....

TANGIBLE ELEMENT OF 'PACKAGE'

What do customers expect?	What do they receive?	What is the quality gap?

INTANGIBLE ELEMENTS OF 'PACKAGE'

What do customers expect?	What do they receive?	What is the quality gap?

EXERCISE 4.2 ACTION PLAN FOR QUALITY

STEP 1 Taking the information which appeared in the third column (quality gap) in Exercise 4.1, convert it into a list of actionable objectives.

It is often helpful to start the wording of each objective with the expression 'We need to ...'; for example, 'We need to improve our guarantee conditions so that they extend for a further six months.' As each objective is listed, give it a number.

STEP 2 Consider the value of each of these objectives in terms of customer satisfaction (use a 0–10 scale, where 10 infers an extremely high level of customer satisfaction).

Also estimate the cost of implementing each of the objectives listed in step 1.

STEP 3 Place each of the objectives in the appropriate quadrant of the following matrix. (*Note*: only the objective numbers that were designated in Step 1 need appear).

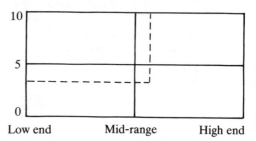

Cost of implementation

STEP 4 Develop an action plan based around just those objectives which fall into the top left-hand quadrant of the matrix, i.e., high value to the customer, low cost to the company.

If funds are available, extend this plan to embrace further objectives which are close to this quadrant, as the dotted line suggests, concentrating on those objectives which provide the higher satisfaction to customers.

EXERCISE 4.3 MAINTAINING A CUSTOMER FOCUS

OBJECTIVE The importance of maintaining a customer focus was emphasised in this chapter, since it has a bearing on both the setting of quality standards and the level of service which is provided. Often we find that a company does less than it might on this front, because its horizons are limited from the outset by issues of cost or lack of resources. This exercise is designed to redress the balance somewhat.

PROCEDURE

1   Imagine that costs or lack of resources were not a barrier to what you might do. In these circumstances, what approaches would be particularly suitable for your organisation in terms of monitoring and maintaining a customer focus? (Make brief notes in this space below or on a separate sheet of paper.)

2   Now make a list of the things the company actually does to maintain a customer focus.

3   Compare the two sets of information you have generated above. The items in response to 1 represent the *ideal* your company should aim for. Those in 2 are the actual approaches used.

   Clearly, you do not have the luxury of limitless resources and so the ideal might always remain out of reach. However, with creative thinking, more effective targeting, savings from non-effective methods, etc., it ought to be possible to move closer towards the ideal without necessarily spending more.

   Reflect on the gaps between 1 and 2 above, and:

   a) Speculate on ways in which approaches could be used which would get closer to the ideal, without incurring great costs.

   b) Test your ideas on colleagues to find out if they believe these to be feasible, and also if they can see ways to make your initial ideas even more powerful.

EXERCISE 4.4 IMPROVING STAFF INVOLVEMENT

OBJECTIVE It was explained that staff involvement was one of the cornerstones of TQM. However, it is impossible to be specific about the best way to achieve this, for what will work well in one company might prove to be a dismal failure in another. Whatever the final choice of method, it must hold the prospect of achieving tangible results, while at the same time exciting and thus motivating the staff themselves.

PROCEDURE In order to come up with a creative approach, it is suggested that groups of employees are invited to brainstorm the subject, thereby providing a range of possibilities from which to pick the most appropriate way forward. (*Note*: for those not familiar with this technique, brief notes are provided after this exercise.)

   Here are some suggestions which might get the brainstorming session off to a good start.

- Award prizes for providing excellent service.
- Set up a suggestion scheme with huge prizes.
- Let staff accompany sales personnel on customer visits.
- Let staff help to run exhibition stands.
- Have poster campaign.
- Have a day where nobody can say 'Yes, but'.
- Involve staff with customers in sorting out complaints.
- Invite customers to speak on training programmes.
- Get people to swap jobs/departments for a day.
- Have proportion of pay related to customer service.
- Get small teams of staff to act as customer service/ quality 'consultants' in other departments.

Try to get at least thirty additional ideas.

BRAINSTORMING is an idea-generating technique developed in the 1950s. It embodies three guiding principles:

- People can be more creative if they stop being critical of their ideas.
- The collective brain-power of a group can out-perform that of an individual.
- The more ideas that can be generated, the higher the chances of finding a world-beater.

Facilities required: A room, free from outside distractions, capable of seating a group of about eight to ten people (best size) in an informal arrangement (such as a semi-circle), together with a flip chart or equivalent, pens, chalks, etc.

Key roles: A non-authoritarian leader to stimulate the session, and a scribe who can write quickly and legibly.

Introduction: Leader explains 'rules' which are:

1 Aim is to generate as many ideas as possible.
2 Ideas are not to be judged, they will be evaluated later.
3 Anything goes, no matter how silly or outrageous ideas might seem at the time.
4 Quality comes out of quantity.

Warm up session: Object is to get people relaxed and in the right frame of mind. Take 20–30 minutes. Have a dummy run on new uses for an everyday object, for example, a coin, clothes peg, pencil, etc. Generate as many ideas as possible which are listed on a flip chart as they emerge.

Debrief: Find out how people felt about the dummy run and the positive points that can be carried into the exercise proper. Measure the idea-generating rate, i.e., ideas divided by time.

Brainstorming session: Define task, for example, 'Ways in which staff involvement can add value to the customer service/quality we provide.' Make sure it is clearly understood. Run as per dummy session, plus any improvements that it disclosed. Aim to improve dummy run generating rate. (*Note*: an experienced group can generate approximately 150 ideas in 20 minutes.)

■ If idea flow dries up, try having a short break.

After session: Get the list of ideas typed up and sent to all participants with some indication of how and when it will be evaluated. Let participants know the results of the evaluation as soon as possible.

Warning: Many managers claim to know all about brainstorming and so they miss out the warm up session. Even top athletes do not race without warming up first. Also authoritarian leadership does not create the relaxed climate essential for a technique like this.

5 *Tuning up the organisation*

In much the same way that one's car performs more efficiently if it is regularly serviced and checked out, so organisations can benefit from equivalent attention. As with the car, the organisation can suffer wear and tear coping with the stresses and strains of workaday life. Its 'fuel pipes' can get clogged, its 'spark plugs' might need renewal, its 'carburettor' might need adjustment and the 'suspension' might have lost its former resilience. Of course this analogy is not perfect, because with the organisation we are talking about people and not mechanical parts. Nevertheless, when put under pressure the organisation will show a similar inclination to break down.

In this chapter we will be considering how managers might take steps to ensure that customer service continues to be 'roadworthy' and performs at a high level. In the course of doing this the manager will be introduced to ideas to help him or her with this important task. The first of these we call the 'customer service-ometer'.

THE 'CUSTOMER SERVICEOMETER'

Before people rush out to buy one, we should point out that such an instrument doesn't really exist. Even so, as we shall see, by using some inventive visualisation we can obtain some valuable information about our level of customer service.

Just imagine that this fabulous instrument was available and that it operated something like a thermometer. However, instead of registering temperature it measured customer service. What would happen if it was plugged into your organisation? What reading

Figure 5.1 The 'customer serviceometer'

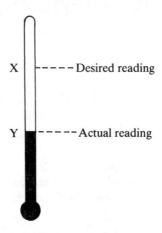

X ├ – – – – Desired reading

Y ├ – – – – – Actual reading

would it give? The chances are that the results would be something like those shown in Figure 5.1. In a similar way that we have a normal blood temperature, so a company can have a desired level of customer service. (It is of course the company's choice regarding where this level is set.) In the illustration this level is X. Exactly what the units of measurement are called is not of import-ance. (Many possibilities spring to mind, how about plaudits?) What is significant, however, is that the 'customer serviceometer' has recorded a level of only Y, which falls short of the desired reading.

This raises two extremely interesting questions for the company:

1   Why is the actual reading lower than desired?
2   Why hasn't the actual reading fallen lower than it has?

Both of these questions are equally important, but in our experi-ence companies frequently omit to ask themselves the second one. As we can see in Figure 5.2, the answers to these questions lie in the fact that there are two sets of forces at work. There are the negative forces which have the effect of pushing performance down and the positive forces which tend to push performance to higher levels.

The 'serviceometer' reading at any given time indicates the

Figure 5.2 The force field

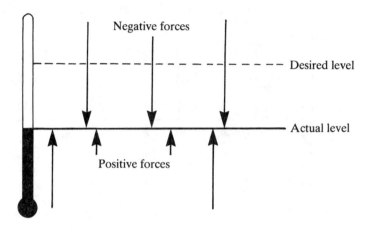

relative balance between the two sets of opposing forces. The fact that the reading hasn't plummeted to zero is because although some things might be going wrong, there is also much which is going right. For example, the company might offer a very competitive range of products or services, the staff could be highly motivated and perhaps the organisation is very market-orientated. By looking for what is going wrong and over-focusing on their weaknesses, companies can often misjudge their strengths.

Of course, there will always be negative forces. Perhaps customer service is not properly co-ordinated, or there might be specific weak links in the chain. These gaps in the provision of customer service are the things which will depress performance.

Some readers will have spotted that the 'serviceometer' is another way of applying the so-called 'Force Field Theory' developed by the social psychologist Kurt Lewin. What makes it particularly appropriate as a diagnostic tool is that it sets few boundaries on the part of the user. It also has a built-in facility to help design a strategy for improvement.

At first sight, to restore performance to its desired level would appear to require a dual strategy of adding to the positive forces, while reducing the negative ones. It has been found, however, that most improvement is achieved by merely removing or reducing the negative forces. Imagine a cork held under water. The easiest way

Figure 5.3 The force field with scoring

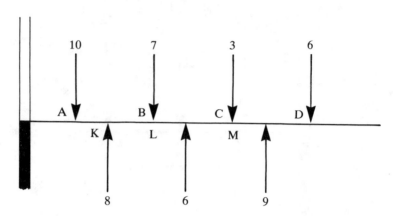

of restoring it to the surface would be to remove the weight which holds it down; its natural buoyancy does the rest. It would be impossible to add properties to the water which would achieve the same results.

Recognising the negative forces and finding ways to diminish their influence is thus the major task facing those managing customer service. Like a good gardener, they have to remove all the weeds and pests that could endanger the natural, healthy growth of the prized plant.

To make the 'serviceometer' information even more useful, it is possible for the manager to apportion different values to the various forces which come into play. As Figure 5.3 shows, a scoring system can be introduced to indicate the weight or importance of the forces of 'light' and 'darkness'. For example, scores can range from 1 to 10, where 10 represents an extremely important issue.

In the example illustrated in Figure 5.3, an improvement strategy could be to leave negative force C alone (since it scores only 3) and instead attack force A vigorously (this scores 10 and so has a greater negative effect). Also, although it is recommended that most energy is put into removing the negative forces, in this example it might be worth examining if there was a way that positive force L might be boosted.

Since every company is different, it is to be expected that the force field diagram which emerges is a unique personal portrait. However, it is our experience that some of the negative forces recur with some regularity in a number of organisations. We will briefly explore the nature of some of these barriers to success.

SOME COMMON BARRIERS

Unawareness

Some companies do little to improve their customer service because they are oblivious of the fact that they need to. They soldier on in blissful ignorance believing that what they do is good enough by any standards. Indeed, the main thrust of this book is to help dismantle this particular barrier. Until companies systematically monitor how they are perceived by their customers and get proper feedback then they are, quite literally, in the dark.

Of course, it is possible to make some random spot checks. One tried and tested method is to try ringing up one's own company with a query and to see how professionally the call is handled by both the switchboard and the relevant department. One of the authors recently rang a local authority department seeking information. The person dealing with the call was extremely polite and concerned, but at one stage had to check some details with another department. 'Just a minute', the person said, 'I will just get this information.' With that the line went dead before there was any chance to point out that the call was long distance. It was some minutes before the cheery voice re-introduced itself, 'Hello! Are you still there? Sorry about the delay but. . . .' From the customer's point of view, how much better it would have been for that person to have explained that there would be delay while the information was found, and check if the caller wanted to hold or be called back.

Equally illuminating can be the process of putting oneself in the customer's shoes and discovering how they are received when they visit your shop, hotel, factory or office. This approach was tried by the manager of an hotel who was interested to investigate how 'user-friendly' his establishment was for disabled people. To do this he spent half a day confined to a wheelchair. The experience was, he confessed afterwards, a 'real eye-opener'. From wrestling with swing doors, to negotiating steps and ways round ill-positioned furniture his pseudo-life was fraught with problems – and it should be explained that this particular hotel had a fine reputation and took pride in the fact that it catered for the disabled.

It is often useful to get a third party to collect information about how the company is perceived by its customers. Their independent position generally enables them to be more objective in seeking out information and thus the company gets very honest feedback from which it can learn. However, it must never be forgotten that the key concern is to learn about customer service, not in absolute terms, but relative to that supplied by one's major competitors.

Organisational inertia

When it comes to introducing change, many organisations appear to possess some sort of 'anti-body' which operates to fight it and maintain the status quo. The more radical the change, the more resistant is the organisation. Exactly where this inertia is centred is difficult to discover. Inevitably there will be parts of the organisation or individuals who, instead of seeing the advantages the change will bring, focus on the disadvantages. This is especially true if they sense that their own power or status will be diminished in some way.

Of course, their opposition is not necessarily voiced openly. Usually a subtle rearguard action is fought which has the effect of dampening down the momentum of the change. So, although there are a range of scenarios for introducing change, as Figure 5.4 illustrates, somehow most acceptable initiatives end up in quadrant 1.

Like the dinosaurs, the larger the organisation, the more difficult it is to get it moving. The extended 'nervous system' takes time to deliver a message from the 'brain'. Indeed, if change is to be managed, a lesson can be learned from these early denizens of our planet. Recent research has speculated that the larger creatures probably had auxiliary hearts in order to be capable of pumping blood around such a huge mass. In a similar way, the organisation will need to ensure that 'pacemakers' are in position so that the necessary changes reach all the organisational nooks and crannies. Such people must be enthusiastic agents of change and be capable of motivating those around them with new ideas. It is not enough to demand change and then expect it to happen. There has also to be an investment in the process of change if organisational inertia is to be overcome.

Figure 5.4 Types of organisational change

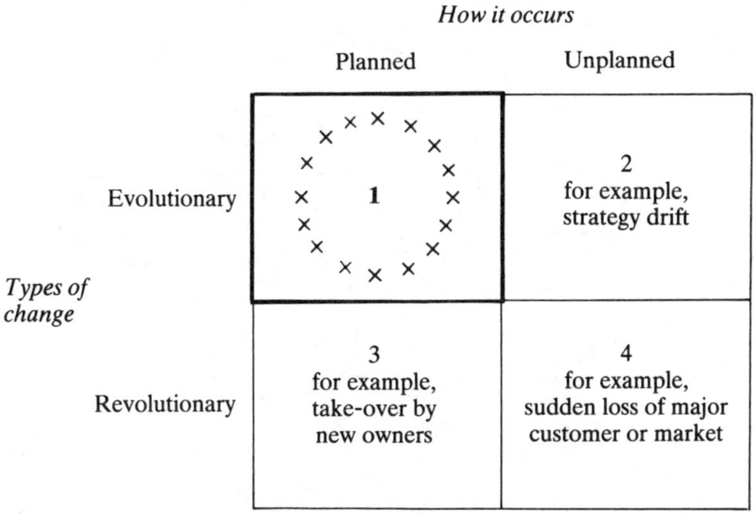

How it occurs

	Planned	Unplanned
Evolutionary	× × × × × × × × × **1** × × × × × × × ×	2 for example, strategy drift
Revolutionary	3 for example, take-over by new owners	4 for example, sudden loss of major customer or market

Types of change

Inappropriate corporate culture

Closely linked to the barrier above is the issue of corporate culture. In their hugely successful book, *In Search of Excellence*, Peters and Waterman[1] concluded that successful companies were those which put emphasis on being 'close to their customers' and having 'an obsession with quality'. Along with these features they noted intensive and active involvement on the part of senior management and a remarkably high people orientation, so much so, that customer relations mirrored employee relations. There was also a high level of measurement and preparedness to receive feedback. At the heart of every successful company they saw a core of shared values to which everyone could feel committed (see Figure 5.5).

If attaining excellence is hard work, it would seem that maintaining it is no easier. Within two years about a third of the companies identified as excellent in the Peters and Waterman study had fallen from grace. It appeared that these stumblers had been unable to adapt to fundamental changes in their markets.

[1]T. Peters and R. Waterman, In Search of Excellence, New York: Harper & Row 1982.

Figure 5.5 Organisation model

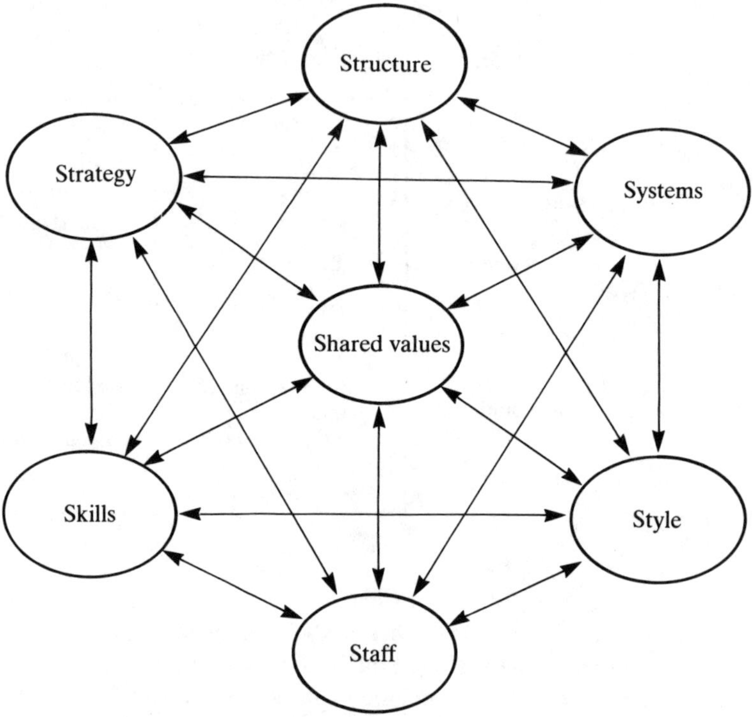

Source: T. Peters and R. Waterman, *In Search of Excellence*, New York: Harper & Row 1982.

They had failed to be sensitive to critical signals from their business environments.

While the model in Figure 5.5 might make eminent good sense and demonstrate how customer service can be integrated into the organisation, it must be recognised that shared values means something more than having a written statement of intent. History shows us that paper has always had the power to deceive: for example, Neville Chamberlain's triumphant return from his meeting with Hitler waving a signed document and proclaiming 'peace in our time'.

People working in organisations are far more practical and down to earth. They look for other signals which tell them what is important or not. These are some of the questions the answers to which tell them what the corporate culture really is.

1　What are the issues to which top management pay most attention, measure and control?

2　How does top management react to critical incidents and crises?

3　What criteria are behind the allocation of rewards, be they financial or status?

4　What criteria lie behind recruitment, selection, promotion and, yes, even dismissal?

5　What things do top management do, for example, by coaching or their general behaviour, which indicate the issues that genuinely excite them?

If customers and customer service feature strongly in this acid test, then it is a fair bet that the organisational culture being transmitted by the leaders will be appropriate. It also follows that if the core culture is supportive of providing high quality customer service, then other things such as organisational structure, systems and procedures and the physical resources will also fall into line.

It is interesting to note in passing that although the above signals are very real and readily picked up by those working in the organisation, they are likely to remain invisible to outsiders such as consultants who might be trying to help the company.

It also follows that the more fundamentally the corporate culture has to change, the more likely it is that new culture carriers will have to replace the old ones. Unless managers can make public the error of their earlier ways and convincingly espouse the new corporate values, there is no room for them in an organisation which seeks to move in a new direction.

Wrong attitudes to customer service

As we can deduce from the discussion above, if there are wrong attitudes to customer service, then it is not necessarily the fault of the people in question, but the management. On the whole, people behave in ways which conform to what they believe the organisation expects of them. Few people enjoy being branded troublemakers. Not only does it make life difficult, but it can also be severely limiting career-wise.

Therefore, while 'wrong attitudes' might be a convenient label to hang on certain people, the situation demands a deeper level of analysis (see Figure 5.6). At the simplest level of analysis people are given advice, for example, 'Always use the customer's name' or 'Speak on the phone with a smile in your voice.' Clearly such an approach is facile and merely cosmetic. Its impact is likely to be equally lightweight.

A deeper level of analysis would be not to give off the cuff advice but to ask the question 'What might these wrong attitudes be saying about the underlying systems and procedures?' For example, how were these people selected? How were they trained? What support are they given by management? What information do they have at their disposal? And so on.

These searching questions might well throw light on why the wrong attitudes exist. Furthermore, they make it clear that any improvements of consequence will only come about if these systems and procedures change. By taking action at level 2, as it is shown in Figure 5.6, a more lasting solution can be expected than for level 1. However, it is equally true that it will be more time consuming to work at this deeper level.

Figure 5.6 Level of analysis and action

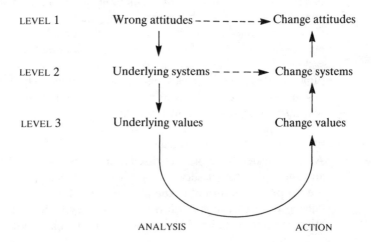

LEVEL 1	Wrong attitudes – – – – – – – ➤ Change attitudes	
LEVEL 2	Underlying systems – – – – ➤ Change systems	
LEVEL 3	Underlying values	Change values

ANALYSIS   ACTION

It is possible to take this analysis one step further still and ask the question 'What do the systems and procedures tell us about the corporate values?' The telling will not necessarily be explicit, but nevertheless can be identified by those who care to listen. For example, do the information systems, regardless of what management might say, indicate that secrecy and not openness is the order of the day? Similarly, is the training process designed to deliver organisational clones or people who will use their individual initiative?

It could be that this level of analysis will show that some of the subterranean values of the organisation might have to change before it is possible to design appropriate systems. In other words, we may be back to changing the corporate culture. The wrong attitudes were merely a manifestation of a deeper malaise. However, anyone working at this level of organisational change, level 3 as it is described in Figure 5.6, is faced with a significantly more difficult task than operating at level 2.

This helps to explain why many companies are prepared to make changes at a systems level and hope that it does the trick. It also explains why this strategy for change often fails to deliver what it promises. Nothing will act better to change wrong attitudes than for top management to create the right environment and to provide positive role models. Some leadership from the front can work wonders.

Lack of involvement

This can happen in one of two ways:

1   Certain members of staff who, by the nature of their work, never come into contact with customers and as a result believe that customer service is the concern of others. We will come back to say more about this group later in this chapter (p. 89).
2   Some members of staff feel (or indeed are) peripheral to the organisation and because of this do not feel actively involved in customer service. It is this group that will be addressed first.

As organisations have slimmed down, as it is euphemistically put, to survive in the recent recession-haunted years, some fundamental changes have taken place. Most companies now recognise that in order to remain viable and maintain their identity and competitive edge they need a central core of key workers, regardless of their level in the organisation. By definition, if any of these people left, it would be a minor disaster for the company.

In addition to this primary core, there are increasingly a number of subcontracted specialists who do jobs previously covered by the company's own staff. Initially, this affected work like catering services, cleaning and security. Nowadays, it is extending into areas like computer programming, training, personnel and design work. It is a brave person who will predict where this trend will lead.

Indeed, many of these specialist services are provided by erstwhile employees who were encouraged to leave and become 'consultants'. The benefit the company experiences is that it doesn't have to find work for a full-time employee and can instead employ someone for just one or two days a week according to the current workload.

There is a third group comprising the workforce who produce the actual goods or services and whose numbers reflect the size of the output of the organisation. Again, in these uncertain times, there has been a tendency for this group to be reduced and replaced with machines where possible. Where this can't be done there appears to be a preference for using part-time labour, partly for cost and contractual reasons and partly for the convenience and flexibility. Thus, for example, a DIY superstore will operate through the week with its core staff, and at the busiest times, weekends and Bank Holidays, part-time staff will help out.

However, whereas the core staff are likely to be highly committed to the organisation and can be motivated by the prospect of promotion or some equivalent career move, the part-time workforce has no such ambition. This is not to say that the part-timers are not interested in doing a good job or that they are lazy, merely that they are different from full-time staff. Indeed, it is not unusual for part-timers to be holding down another job elsewhere, be it full-time or part-time. They might even be better educated and more highly qualified that the permanent staff. Quite understandably, with such 'semi-attached' staff basic things like training become something of a problem. They don't always receive the same intensive instruction about, for example, product knowledge. As a result, when questioned in depth by customers who are genuinely interested in making a purchase, these staff are often found to be wanting.

Exactly how this group of workers can be made to feel part of the company, when clearly they work under different contractual arrangements from their full-time colleagues, is an on-going management problem. As the example given above illustrates, for no fault of their own, because of their relative lack of involvement with the company and its identity, such staff can often be the Achilles' heel of the customer service package. While this discussion about involvement has focused on part-timers, it must not be forgotten that some managements treat their full-time staff in such a cavalier and off-hand way that they alienate them. Those who indulge in such negative tactics deserve to reap their just rewards. Management by stupidity is not a style which holds much promise of success.

Companies which think more positively about the problems of keeping their staff involved and feeling part of a drive towards better customer service are prepared to experiment until they find a formula which works for them. The chances are that there is no single approach which will, like magic, lead to the promised land. It is more a matter of intelligent hard work leading to success. As we have seen, it is up to management to establish a culture in which customer service can flourish. If this prerequisite is achieved, then various campaigns to stimulate staff regarding customer service can play a valuable part in increasing their involvement. Equally, well thought out suggestions schemes or approaches similar to those developed for quality circles can also bring success.

These, then, are some of the barriers which can feature in the force field diagram. Of course, there will be others such as lack of resources or lack of skills, but on the whole those are more obvious and, damaging though they might be, don't have quite the same insidious effects on customer service.

Staff who never deal with customers

For most organisations, the number of staff who don't actually deal with customers directly, either face-to-face or over the telephone, will greatly outnumber those who do. This can sometimes present a problem in that customer service is only seen to be the province of those at the so-called sharp end. With this type of mind-set, those who exclude themselves are perhaps at best indifferent to the issue of customer service.

Closer examination will, of course, show that everyone has a contribution to make in ensuring that customer service of the desired level is provided. From the person who buys raw materials or component parts, to the machine operator, to the packer, all can make a contribution to the final product quality and its presentation. In this sense, all the support services, albeit indirectly, also make their contribution. Any job in the company should exist only to help provide better products or services. If this underlying *raison d'être* cannot be identified, then serious questions should be asked regarding why such a job position exists. In the present competitive environment, no company can afford to carry passengers. On the contrary, everyone should be encouraged to add value to their output by maintaining the highest standards of performance.

At an intellectual level, this argument can be readily accepted. Unfortunately, this does not mean that it automatically wins over the hearts and minds of all those in the company, many of whom, as we said, see customer service to be the concern only of those in the front-line. In order to make an impact, campaigns and training programmes need to be designed and introduced to create the necessary stimulus.

Training programmes
The rationale behind most training initiatives hinges on three propositions:

1   The company doesn't pay your wages, customers do.
2   We must all do our utmost to ensure that our customers are happy in their dealings with us (the feel good factor) and thereby remain customers and enable us all to face the future with more certainty.
3   If we don't do this better than our competitors we might as well shut up shop.

Such a stark and unambiguous message cannot leave anyone unaware of the importance of becoming increasingly customer-focused. Indeed, many in-company training programmes take this theme for their title. 'Putting People First' was the name used by British Airways for their approach, and no doubt other companies have developed their own versions which add up to a similar concept. Such training programmes are generally inspired by the notion of the value-added chain (see Figures 5.7 and 5.8).

Figure 5.7 shows the ultimate customer for a car as being on the end of a chain of operations which started with somebody extracting metal ore from the ground. Such a chain only remains viable as long as each link presents its output to the next stage in a way that the customer finds acceptable. Each only remains a link while it is adding value to what it receives, while at the same time changing the shape and properties of its input. So, for example, if the customer doesn't like what he is presented with, he will try another dealer. Similarly, now that legislation is changing, the dealer can seek a different manufacturer, and so on down the chain.

The profit that each enterprise makes comes from adding value to its raw input, and that value has to have currency in the customer's terms.

As Figure 5.8 shows, a similar value-added chain operates within the individual company. In an identical way to the whole industry, each person has to 'add value' to the job they perform in order that the salesperson can deliver value to his or her customer.

By accepting the model that Figure 5.8 provides, it follows that everyone in the company has a customer. Moreover, by doing their jobs in a way that provides maximum customer satisfaction they enhance the output of the company and increase overall customer service.

The training programme, then, has to take this concept one step further and get all staff members to:

1   Identify who their customers are.
2   Find out what they have been doing in their work that the customer finds helpful and would like to see happen more often.

Figure 5.7 The value-added chain for cars

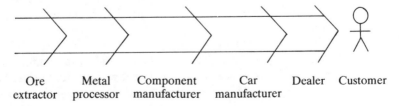

Ore   Metal   Component   Car   Dealer   Customer
extractor   processor   manufacturer   manufacturer

Figure 5.8 The 'in-company' value-added chain (example only)

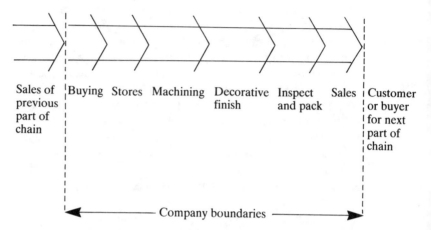

Sales of   Buying Stores Machining Decorative Inspect   Sales Customer
previous   finish   and pack   or buyer
part of   for next
chain   part of
                                                                      chain

◄─────────── Company boundaries ───────────►

3   Find out what things need to carry on at about the same level.
4   Find out what things cause the customer problems and ought
    to be eliminated or reduced.
5   Develop a personal improvement plan on the basis of this
    information.

While this might sound easy and straightforward on the surface, it
can have far-reaching implications in the company. For example,
many managers have not stopped to think who their customers are.
Often they are his or her own staff, who are dependent upon the
manager to provide the necessary information or resources in
order to fulfil their job role. Thus, this approach can challenge the
old order: for example, it can turn existing top-down appraisal
schemes on their head.

  Whatever else it might achieve, this tough yet realistic approach
releases energy and uncovers many hitherto unknown problems.
Above all, it assuredly lays the ghost that 'customer service is
nothing to do with me'.

  The lasting benefit of this type of customer service training is
that the way people deal with each other within the company
becomes a mirror of the way they deal with those outside. We are
not talking about just being nice to people, but genuinely trying to

help them. Thus, the whole concept of customer service becomes a reality, not a mere façade. The ogre-like Mr Hyde within the company does not have to undergo a transformation into the nice Dr Jekyll in order to speak to a customer. Because of the drive to treat one's customers with respect and genuine concern, be they inside or outside the company, even chance contacts do nothing to damage the company's image and reputation.

The one underlying assumption with all of these types of programmes is that customers are always rational and reasonable. Sadly, experience tells us that this is not always the case. For this reason, those people who come into regular contact with customers sometimes need additional training to help them deal with the awkward and often downright rude people who occasionally cross their path.

SPECIALIST TRAINING

Most of these types of training programmes are in the domain of interpersonal skills. To look in-depth at some of the different approaches is beyond the remit of this book. Nevertheless, for the sake of completeness, we give brief explanations of some of the more common themes developed in staff training.

Active listening

Although listening plays a key part in communications, very few people have had lessons in it in the same way as for writing, reading and even speaking. Active listening is the name for a technique in which the listener not only hears the words the customer is saying, but construes their real meaning by observing other signals such as tone of voice and emphasis. To ensure that the genuine message has been picked up, the listener reflects back to the customers in a summarised form what he or she has understood. This approach ensures that the conversation progresses on the basis of what the customer is really saying, not what the listener thinks he or she is saying. By doing this misunderstandings and confusion are avoided.

Body language

Much of what people communicate is natural and unspoken. The smile that says 'I'm pleased to see you', the set face that says 'I'm angry', the slumped posture that says 'I'm whacked', are all examples of body language. On the whole 'people' people, that is to say those with highly developed social skills, are more astute at reading body language and equally adept at using it.

However, understanding body language is a skill which most of us possess, even if it has lain dormant for some time. Clearly, for those who have face-to-face dealings with customers, 'reading' the unspoken messages greatly adds to their chances of establishing communication and avoiding unproductive detours.

Assertiveness training

It is claimed that behaviour can be placed in three basic categories, which broadly speaking can be described as:

1   Aggressive – when the individual's need to be heard or noticed becomes paramount, to the exclusion of the needs of others.
2   Passive – when the individual subjugates his or her own needs and wants to those of the other person.
3   Assertive – which is a middle path between those two extremes. Thus the assertive person will own up to what he or she wants out of a situation, but not in a way that renders the other person powerless.

People are inclined to operate in one of these categories most of the time, in a similar way that we might prefer to wear a favourite pair of shoes more frequently than others. Equally, there can be particular situations which cause a person to stop being 'themselves'.

Assertive behaviour is seen to be the most productive of the three types, because it alone provides a context for meeting others as equals in an open and frank way. By choosing to be assertive when faced with, say, an aggressive complaining customer, the individual will be better placed to avoid getting dragged into a slanging match and will be able to restore the situation to some semblance of order.

Transactional analysis (TA)

This is an approach based on the work of the Canadian psychologist Eric Berne. He maintained that transactions between two people can be analysed in terms of their 'ego states' of which there are three. He called these parent, adult and child. The significance of these somewhat pejorative labels is that each represents an ensemble of beliefs and behaviours which have a bearing upon how we interact with the people and situations which go to make up our personal worlds.

The 'parent' is said to be the collected values, attitudes, behaviours and general rules for living, *copied from* parent figures in our formative years. According to Berne, these stay in our personal computer (the brain) and influence our behaviour. Thus, whenever we are called upon to criticise, cajole, comfort, instruct, counsel and so on, much of how we act is due to these old tapes playing back, regardless of how valid they might be for the situation. Words like don't, ought, must, should, no and shouldn't, figure strongly in the parent ego state vocabulary.

The 'child' ego state is a similar collection of things from that early period of life, but this time the feelings, attitudes and behaviours which resulted from *responding to* parental behaviour. Such feelings include excitement, fear, helplessness, dependency, joy, playfulness and so on. Again certain situations or people can cause these old tapes to play back and influence our present day behaviour.

The 'adult' ego state comprises feelings, attitudes and behaviours associated with gathering information, analysing it and solving problems. In a sense, the adult is a kind of data processor which computes information based on the real life data. Thus the adult vocabulary is typified by questions such as why? where? how? when?, etc., and unemotional statements of fact.

One way of regarding these three ego states is that of:

1   the parent   =   the taught concept of life
2   the child   =   the felt concept of life
3   the adult   =   the thought-out concept of life.

Conventionally in TA an individual is represented as shown in Figure 5.9a, but in reality the ego states might not be in such equilibrium, or so clearly defined (see Figures 5.9b and c). Understanding the personality make-up in Berne's terms makes it possible to analyse transactions between individuals. For example, suppose a shopper brought back a faulty article. The transaction might be as shown in Figure 5.10. Here it was possible to achieve

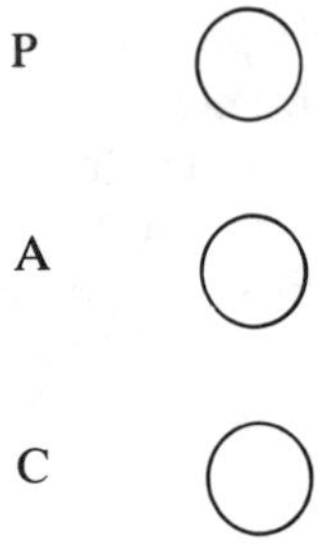

Figure 5.9a
Normal
representation of
personality

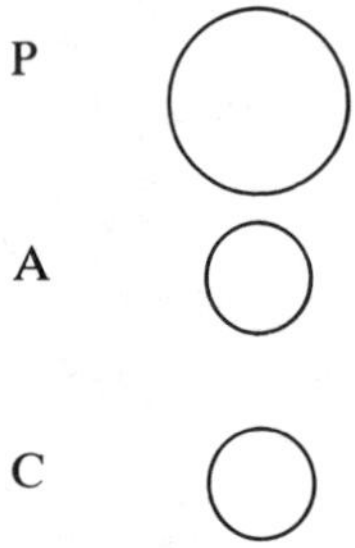

Figure 5.9b
Parent-dominated
personality (any ego
state can be dominant)

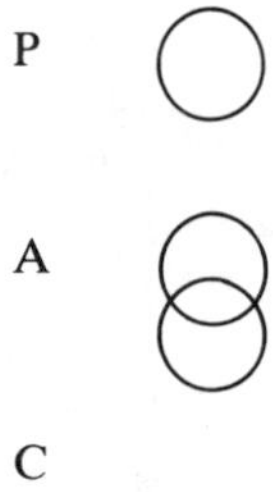

Figure 5.9c
Adult contaminated
by child (parent may
also contaminate the
adult)

something in the transaction because it was between the two
'adults'. However, the assistant's response could have been
different, and this is shown diagrammatically in Figure 5.11. In
situation (a) the assistant did not respond from the adult ego state
as expected, but from the parent. Furthermore, the assistant
addressed the remark to the shopper's child. In (b), the assistant
responded from the child and perceived the shopper to be a critical
parent. In TA terms both of these were crossed transactions (as the
arrows show), unlike the first example which was parallel.
Communication difficulties always arise from crossed transactions
because the two parties are virtually speaking a different and un-
expected language.

Of course, the transaction could be further complicated by the
shopper starting off like this:

c) 'When I come to a shop like this I don't expect to be palmed
off with rubbish. I insist on seeing the manager!' (Parent).
d) 'I don't want to bother you, I can see you that you are busy,
but I've got a bit of a problem' (Child).

So every transaction has a wide range of possibilities in terms of
who is actually talking to whom.

All of us have the capability of using our parent, adult or child

Figure 5.10 An adult–adult transaction

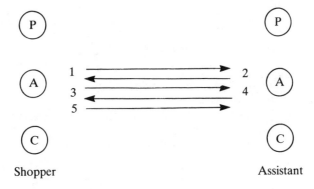

Shopper   Assistant

1 *Shopper:* I bought this electric kettle here yesterday and found it to be faulty when I tried to use it.
2 *Assistant:* What was the trouble?
3 *Shopper:* The indicator didn't light up and the water remained cold. It was certainly switched on.
4 *Assistant:* Would you like a replacement or your money back?
5 *Shopper:* A replacement please.

Figure 5.11 Examples of crossed transactions

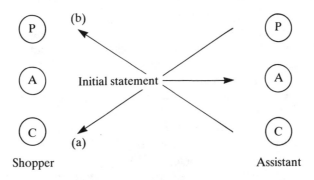

Shopper   Assistant

a) Well, it was alright when it left here, we only sell the highest quality kitchen equipment. You probably mistreated it (Parent). Or,
b) Don't blame me. I didn't make it (Child).

ego states at will. The parent helps us to control and nurture, the child to wheedle, manipulate, have fun and be creative, the adult to be analytical, make decisions and generally get 'the business' done.

Only adult–adult transactions achieve positive results, all others are either due to misreadings of situations or a willingness to indulge the inappropriate ego state.

By learning how to recognise ego states in oneself and other people at times when communication is going awry, the individual can rescue the situation and restore it to a productive level. The ability to do this stops the transaction from degenerating into a sterile routine pattern or 'game' as Berne defines it.

TA can be very helpful to those who have face-to-face dealings with customers. It is an approach which is relatively easy to understand and one which has applications to many other aspects of organisational and personal life.

These then are just some of the approaches which can be introduced into interpersonal skills training programmes for those who deal with customers. Of course, it is essential that they are combined with training about product knowledge. To be competent in one area to the exclusion of the other is no way to run a business.

ACTION PLANNING

In this chapter we have considered various aspects of the organisation where some form of improvement planning could prove to be of benefit. However, in order to ensure that the changes introduced make maximum impact, they will need to be clearly understood and sequenced in the most logical manner. Often enabling objectives have to be achieved before the primary issues can be tackled.

In order to ensure that all the organisational issues regarding customer service are considered and put into an overall context it is useful to complete a SWOT type of analysis. For those not familiar with this expression, it is an acronym of the initial letters of strengths, weaknesses, opportunities and threats. By collecting all data and grouping them under these headings it becomes possible to see at a glance what the key issues are.

Another advantage of using a SWOT approach is that regardless of the depth of analysis, all departments (indeed everybody in the organisation) could provide information regarding how they perceive the customer service that is provided. This being the case, it follows that all parts of the organisation can be requested to provide SWOTs of their own contribution to customer service, as well as how they see the corporate effort.

By getting staff involved in this way, not only is a rich lode of information mined, but also it creates an added interest and awareness about the company's intentions to improve customer service. It is therefore a useful method for providing staff motivation without having to resort to financial inducements or costly gimmicks.

Of course, the SWOT analysis will vary from company to company, although some common issues might tend to be raised as we have suggested earlier in this book. An example of how it might appear is shown in Figure 5.12. This shows a fairly simple SWOT analysis developed by a tyre and exhaust systems outlet. What is immediately apparent is that this small company has quite a lot going for it in terms of its strengths. Moreover, its weaknesses should be relatively easy to overcome given some modest investment, some imaginative thinking and some staff training.

The main cloud on the horizon is the threat of a 'national' setting up a competing unit that has the potential of advertising more heavily and pricing at a discount. In fact, to counter this threat provides an added impetus to improve service and by doing so increase customer loyalty and a 'word-of-mouth' local network.

An improvement plan could be designed using a type of critical path technique. Alternatively something like the 'how–how' diagram, as shown in Figure 5.13, could be used.

This approach helps to identify the steps that need to be taken in order to implement a solution. By asking the question 'How?' as each activity is flagged, an action route becomes clear and is made explicit. 'How?' is continually asked until to go any further makes no obvious sense. It operates in much the same way as the 'why?–why?' diagram that was introduced in Chapter 3.

The 'how–how' approach can be particularly useful if tackled by a team. The discussions it raises as the diagram develops can help to overcome and settle differences of opinion. It is obviously preferable that divergent views should be sorted out at this early stage, rather than later when they could be costly to accommodate.

Figure 5.12 An example of SWOT analysis for a local tyre and exhaust fitting service

Strengths	*Weaknesses*
■ Easy access/good location ■ Low staff turnover ■ Good reputation ■ Competitive prices ■ Good quality workmanship	■ Untidy reception area ■ Noisy and dirty customer waiting room ■ Delays in answering phone ■ Don't make best use of customer information, for example, use name or mail-shot special offers ■ External appearance of premises not welcoming
Opportunities	*Threats*
■ Legislation on tyre wear and exhaust emissions means greater frequency of replacement ■ Tie up with local garage for all tyre and exhaust fitting ■ Competitor retiring	■ National outlet to open branch nearby ■ Economic situation encouraging DIY repairs and 'cowboys'

It must be emphasised that the illustration provided in Figure 5.13 is merely an example and is not intended to be copied as a general prescription. Like most of the other ideas in this book, the 'how–how' diagram has to be applied to a specific company situation. It then becomes a unique record of what actions can be taken.

SUMMARY

In this final chapter we have looked at ways to keep the organisation operating at a consistently high level when it comes to providing customer service. We have seen that it was important to monitor on a regular basis the positive and negative forces that

Figure 5.13 The 'how–how' diagram (example)

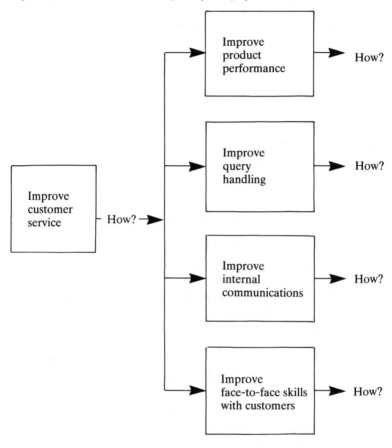

come into play. Moreover, it has been shown that the removal of the negative forces is likely to be the best strategy for bringing about improvement.

We then looked at some of the more common barriers to customer service which appear to affect many companies. These are unawareness, organisational inertia, inappropriate corporate culture, wrong attitudes to customer service and lack of involvement. There has been also some discussion about ways to tackle these areas, particularly the issue about staff who do not see customer service to be their responsibility.

The chapter finished by looking at various training approaches and the need to have an overall plan for improving customer service. That is to say, a plan which takes into account the need for scheduling activities in an optimal way, thereby maximising the benefits they bring.

POSTSCRIPT

A couple of years ago someone on a course handed one of the authors the following piece of prose. We have been unable to trace its origins and conclude it was written by the ubiquitous Anon. It expresses succinctly the viewpoint of the customer and because all of us are customers at various times, its truth is self-evident.

I am your customer

I am your customer. Satisfy my wants – add personal attention and a friendly touch – and I will become a walking advertisement for your products and services. Ignore my wants, show carelessness, inattention and poor manners, and I will simply cease to exist – as far as you are concerned.

I am sophisticated. Much more so than I was a few years ago. My needs are more complex. I have grown accustomed to better things. I have money to spend. I am an egotist. I am sensitive; I am proud. My ego needs the nourishment of a friendly, personal greeting from you. It is important to me that you appreciate my business. After all, when I buy your products and services, my money is feeding you.

I am a perfectionist. I want the best I can have for the money I spend. When I criticise your products or service – and I will, to anyone who will listen when I am dissatisfied – then take heed. The source of my discontent lies in something you or the products you sell have failed to do. Find that source and eliminate it or you will lose my business and that of my friends as well.

I am fickle. Other businessmen continually beckon to me with offers of 'more for my money'. To keep my business, you must offer something better than they. I am your customer now, but you must prove to me again and again that I have made a wise choice in selecting you, your products and services above all others.

By taking this message on board, and by providing a higher level of customer service than its rivals, a company can establish and sustain a competitive advantage over them. However, for their part, competitors, being neither stupid nor lazy, will not just sit back inanimately. They too will seek to establish some form of competitive edge. Thus the scene is set for a period of high activity and creativity in the field of customer service. As in other walks of life, the battles will not necessarily be won by the largest armies, but by the smartest generals. At the end of the day the only limits on customer service are those imposed by our imagination and our willingness to break new ground in the search for excellence.

EXERCISE 5.1 THE 'CUSTOMER SERVICEOMETER'

PROCEDURE

1   Using the ideas put forward in this chapter, develop a force field diagram showing the driving and restraining forces which influence the provision of customer service. Draw the arrows so that the greater the influence, the longer the length.

Restraining forces

Current level _____

Driving forces

2   From the completed diagram above, devise the outline of an improvement strategy which, in particular, sets out to remove or reduce the major restraining forces.

EXERCISE 5.2 CUSTOMER SERVICE – ORGANISATIONAL ISSUES

PROCEDURE What follows is a series of statements about your organisation's approach to customer service. You are asked to score each statement as follows:

If you strongly disagree	score −2
If you tend to disagree	score −1
If you are unsure if you agree or disagree	score 0
If you tend to agree	score 1
If you strongly agree	score 2

Please only enter your score in the position indicated by the dotted line next to the statement. Since this exercise is an attempt to obtain genuine and useful information about your organisation, please try to be as accurate and objective as you can as you complete the questionnaire.

	A	B	C	D	E
1 Top management show an active interest in customer service					.....
2 Top management demonstrate their understanding of customer service		.....			
3 Top management use customer service information as a basis for making key marketing decisions				.....	
4 Top management allocate sufficient resources to ensure that customer service can function at the appropriate level			.....		
5 The need for good customer service is clearly explained to all levels of staff		.....			

	A	B	C	D	E
6 There is adequate information/ hard data upon which to base a customer service plan		.....			
7 There is a high degree of co-operation between departments when it comes to issues relating to customer service				.....	
8 People are clear about the role they play when it comes to customer service				.....	
9 Department managers clearly understand the company's overall strategy for customer service			.....		
10 Department managers believe that customer service is important					.....
11 Enough time is devoted to improving customer service				.....	
12 Department managers are all given training in customer service			.....		
13 Customer service never suffers for the lack of resources				.....	
14 It is reasonable for a company like ours to have a well thought out approach to customer service					.....
15 Reasons for our successes and failures in customer service are regularly appraised				.....	
16 Customer service isn't just left to the specialists, all managers can make a valuable contribution				.....	
17 Our organisational style encourages and makes it easy to provide a high level of customer service					.....

	A	B	C	D	E
18 There is a clear understanding about the organisation's objectives regarding customer service	.....				
19 Customer service opportunities are highlighted by regular review sessions			.....		
20 All functional specialists contribute to sessions relating to customer service				.....	
21 We limit our customer service activities so that we don't have to attempt to do too many things at one time			.....		
22 Being involved in customer service is good for one's career in our company, or brings financial rewards					.....
23 Only essential data are collected for customer service				.....	
24 Customer service does not operate in an 'ivory tower'				.....	
25 From the wealth of customer information available to us we are good at identifying the most important issues			.....		
26 There is a good balance between anecdotal evidence and hard data in our approach to customer service			.....		
27 All staff play their part in delivering customer service				.....	
28 Our customer service programme demonstrates an awareness of competitor activity		.....			

	A	B	C	D	E
29 The inputs to our customer service analysis are on the whole as accurate as we can get them		.....			
30 Customer service is tackled in a serious and professional manner				.....	
31 In trying to provide a high level of customer service we don't duck major problems it might raise in the organisation					.....
32 There is great attention to detail in our approach to customer service	.....				
33 We recognise that we need to match our capabilities with the expectations of our customers if we are to provide the service levels they require			.....		
34 All managers should be concerned with making suggestions and finding ways to improve customer service					.....
35 Customer service is a priority issue in our organisation					.....
36 'Feedback' about current customer service is not 'massaged' in order to make it more acceptable to top management			.....		
37 Staff (on the whole) understand and are reasonably happy that our approach to customer service is both logical and appropriate	.....				
38 Customer service is integrated into the marketing plan and operates on the same overall time-scale				.....	

	A	B	C	D	E
39 What we set out to achieve in customer service is seen as the start of a long-term improvement plan, not a 'one-off' cure-all				.....	
40 Top management are as bound to our customer service objectives as all other members of the organisation				.....	
41 The 'champions' of customer service are sufficiently high in the organisation that they can influence policy-making				.....	
42 People are always given clear instructions regarding the nature of their expected contribution to customer service			.....		
43 Data collection and retrieval about customer service issues are kept as simple as possible				.....	
44 Our customer service plans are essentially practical and quite unambiguous, without going into great detail				.....	
45 When people have a specialist role to play in customer service it is made quite clear to them				.....	
46 We are always prepared to use new techniques or to invest more in our approaches to customer service			.....		
47 Customer service has a high priority throughout the organisation					.....
48 Specific research studies (either			.....		

		A	B	C	D	E

internal or external) are often
used as inputs to our appraisals of
our customer services programmes

49 Customer service is regularly   .....
   evaluated in the search for
   improved performance

50 Top management monitor   .....
   customer service and assess that
   progress is on track

Now add up the total scores for
each column

A	B	C	D	E

Interpretation

It can be shown that customer service can suffer for a number
of reasons. Some of the key organisational barriers can be:

A Cognitive, that is to say people are unaware or have
   insufficient knowledge to be effective.

B Lack of resources, such as time, data, people, etc.

C Inappropriate systems and procedures.

D Role confusion, people are not clear of the roles they are
   expected to play, or the way they relate to each other is
   not productive.

E The general climate is not really supportive of customer
   service.

In fact the questionnaire columns A–E represent the barriers
listed above. Because of the way the scoring is organised it is
possible to score each column between −20 and +20. In this
questionnaire, the higher the score, the less that particular
issue is a barrier to better customer service.

In other words, the columns with low scores (certainly any below 0) will be the areas worth investigating initially in the search for improvement. Within those columns it will be useful to pay particular attention to the individual statements which scored −2.

Personal notes

List the actions that need to be taken as a result of the information provided by this questionnaire.

EXERCISE 5.3 GETTING FEEDBACK FROM THE STAFF

OBJECTIVE In order to provide excellent customer service it is important that the company's staff are as equally committed to the concept as senior management. Therefore, it is valuable to check, on a regular basis, how the staff perceive their day-to-day work and its immediate environment (in terms of the support, encouragement and constraints it provides).

If, on the whole, the staff sense that the company is organised in a way that encourages behaviour which is directed towards satisfying customers' needs, that is clearly a good omen. What is equally true is that if staff perceive that they are being treated unfairly and that conflict rather than co-operation typifies the work situation, then being 'nice' to customers has a hollow ring to it. Like charity, putting people first has to start at home.

PROCEDURE The questionnaire provided below is merely an example of how staff opinion can be elicited. It may not necessarily pose all the questions that are pertinent to every organisation, but it can be tailored to suit most situations.

Once the process of getting staff feedback is under way, it is desirable to continue it on a regular basis, say once a year. In this way it becomes possible to monitor if the organisational 'black spots' have been eradicated by either training or the redesign of jobs and systems.

Questionnaire

We want to make the company one which is respected for providing quality and customer service. Because this is a task in which everyone has a part to play, we are interested in your opinions about the company as a place to work. Please give your honest opinions to the questions asked here. All staff will be answering the same questions and only overall results will be looked at – you as an individual will remain anonymous. Please bear in mind that we can only bring about improvements at work with your help.

SECTION 1 Background information

(Please tick the appropriate boxes)

1   Male ☐   Female ☐

2   Length of service:

less than 1 year   ☐

1–5 years   ☐

more than 5 years   ☐

3   Functional area:

production ☐   sales/marketing ☐

personnel & training ☐   engineering & resrch ☐

accounts & admin. ☐   stores & distribution ☐

SECTION 2 How to answer

Please write your score in each box as follows:

On the whole tend to agree with statement   score 2
Difficult to say, or not sure   score 1
On the whole, tend to disagree with statement score 0

1   I find my work satisfying   ☐

2   The people I work with help each other when
    there are problems   ☐

3   My supervisor/manager expects excellent
    performance at all times   ☐

4   My supervisor/manager and I always have an
    annual performance review   ☐

5   I am given the opportunity in my job to correct
    mistakes   ☐

6 There is good co-operation between my work group and other work groups ☐

7 Managers with whom I come into contact are trying hard to make the company successful ☐

8 I am encouraged in my job to make suggestions for improvements ☐

9 My job gives me opportunities to solve problems at work ☐

10 People know how their jobs affect customer satisfaction ☐

11 Company policies are applied consistently throughout the company ☐

12 Those with whom I work have a great interest in the company ☐

13 I have ample opportunity to use my skills and abilities in my job ☐

14 My job is such that I can measure my own performance ☐

15 My supervisor/manager is someone I would go to if I had a personal problem or felt I was being treated unfairly ☐

16 I feel that I am part of a team ☐

17 I have confidence in the fairness and honesty of management ☐

18 My supervisor/manager trusts me to do a good job ☐

19 I know how my job fits in with others in the organisation ☐

20 It is easy for me to find out things I need to know to do my job ☐

21 I am kept informed about company plans and new developments ☐

22 I have freedom in my job to use my own judgement and initiative ☐

23 My job is never dull and monotonous ☐

24 There is too much pressure in my job ☐

25 My supervisor/manager takes the time to speak to me frequently at work ☐

26 My supervisor/manager welcomes ideas even when they are different to his/her own ☐

27 We are kept well-informed about things that affect our department ☐

28 People are given good training on new work, equipment, etc. ☐

29 I'm proud to work for the company ☐

30 Good performance is rewarded fairly ☐

31 I see a good future for me in the company ☐

32 Recently (say, during the last six months) I have seriously considered leaving the company ☐

33 My supervisor/manager could give more credit for a job well done ☐

34 We sometimes have to look busy when there isn't enough to do ☐

35 The working conditions for my group (for example, space, heating, etc.) are conducive to good performance ☐

36 My supervisor/manager is open in his/her dealings with me and doesn't play at politics ☐

37 My work group is very flexible and can

accommodate sudden changes of priority with
little fuss and bother ☐

38 My supervisor/manager helps me to learn from
my mistakes ☐

39 This survey approach is a good way to identify
problems which need solving ☐

40 I can recognise the improvements which resulted
from last year's survey ☐

Or if this is the first attempt at this kind of survey:

40 I believe that management will take positive steps
to act on issues disclosed by this survey ☐

Are there any issues you think should have been included in
Section 2 but were not? Please provide brief notes (continue
on another sheet if necessary).

Interpretation

This questionnaire is designed to explore four main areas:

1   How the individual perceives his/her job (questions 1, 5, 8, 9, 13, 14, 20, 22, 23, 24).
2   Issues about the work group (questions 2, 6, 10, 12, 16, 27, 28, 34, 35, 37).
3   How the supervisor/manager is perceived (questions 3, 4, 15, 17, 18, 25, 26, 33, 36, 38).
4   How the company is viewed in general (questions 7, 11, 19, 21, 29, 30, 31, 32, 39, 40).

Thus there is a maximum score of 20 (2 × 10 questions) for each of these areas. (*Note*: the scores for questions 24, 32, 33, 34 need to be reversed, i.e., 0 = 2 and 2 = 0, if collective scores are calculated.) The *lowest* scores indicate the problem areas.

However, what might be more important than the overall analysis could be how different departments, sexes or those with different lengths of service respond to individual questions.

EXERCISE 5.4   SHARED IMPROVEMENT PLANS

OBJECTIVE   Often a subordinate and his/her supervisor could together make a greater contribution to improving customer service if they were both 'pulling in the same direction'. This exercise helps to achieve this.

PROCEDURE

STEP 1   *Separately* the subordinate and supervisor list what they perceive to be the areas of the former's contributions to customer service.

STEP 2   *Together* both compare their lists and agree on a

composite one about which there is no dispute, and which truly reflects the work situation.

STEP 3 *Separately* each prioritise from the composite list the various customer service activities.

STEP 4 *Together* the ranking of the priorities is discussed and differences resolved so that a joint priority list evolves.

STEP 5 *Separately* taking the main priority tasks from the agreed list:
a) The supervisor writes down for the subordinate:
   i) Where and how existing standards should be maintained.
   ii) Where and how improvements might be made.
   iii) Those activities which are consuming too much time and are not very productive and should be reduced.
b) The subordinate writes down for the supervisor:
   i) Where and how existing levels of support should be maintained.
   ii) Where and how more support could be provided and could lead to the subordinate being more productive.
   iii) What actions the supervisor could reduce to make the subordinate's job easier or more productive re customer service.

STEP 6 *Together* the subordinate and supervisor share the above information and negotiate an improvement plan along the lines of 'I will do this and you will do that'. In this way both are committed to improving customer service in priority areas in an agreed way.

Note: This process works best if both parties have a day or so to complete the 'separate' activities. This enables some reflective thought to go into whatever is generated at these stages.

EXERCISE 5.5 CUSTOMER SERVICE AUDIT CHECKLIST

OBJECTIVE The following list is an aid to measure and monitor performance against customer requirements. It captures most of the issues raised in this book and in that sense provides a neat summary of all that has gone before.

PROCEDURE

- Do you have a written customer service policy?
- Is this given a wide circulation within the company?
- Do customers receive a copy of this policy?
- Is customer service included in the marketing plan?
- What elements of customer service do you regularly monitor?
- Do you think other aspects of service should be monitored?
- Do you monitor competitive service performance?
- Do you know the true costs of providing customer service?
- Do customers have direct access to information on stock availability and delivery?
- How do you report to customers on order status?
- Is there a single point of contact for customers in your company?
- Do customers know who this individual is?
- Is any attempt made to estimate the cost of customer service failures (for example, a part delivery, late delivery, etc.)?
- Do you seek to measure the costs of providing different levels of service?
- Do you have internal service measures as well as external measures?
- How do you communicate service policies to customers?
- What is your average order cycle time?
- How does this compare with that of your major competitors?
- Do you monitor actual order-to-delivery lead-time performance?

- Do you have a system for accounting for customer profitability?
- Does the chief executive regularly receive a report on customer service performance?
- Do you consciously seek to hire individuals with a positive attitude towards customer service?
- Does customer service feature in the criteria for staff promotion?
- Do you use quality control concepts in managing customer service?
- Do you differentiate service levels by product?
- Do you differentiate customer service levels by customer type?
- Do you have a standard cost for an out of stock situation (for example, cost of lost sales, cost of back orders, etc.)?
- Do you provide customers with a customer service manual?
- Do you monitor the internal customer service 'climate' on a regular basis?
- Does your customer service organisation effectively manage the client relationship from order to delivery and beyond?
- How do you monitor and respond to complaints?
- How responsive are you to claims from customers?
- Do you allocate adequate resources to the development of customer service?
- How do you seek to maintain a customer focus?
- Does customer service regularly feature at management meetings and in training programmes?
- What specific actions do you take to ensure that staff motivation re customer service is maintained at a high level?
- Is the company image re customer service adequate for the markets in which it operates?

Source: Adapted, with the kind permission of the author, from Martin Christopher, *The Customer Service Planner*, Oxford: Butterworth-Heinemann 1991.

Appendix 1
Cards for Exercise 2.3

Critical for success	Important for success
Fairly important for success	Useful for success
Not applicable for success	Technical competence
Quality	Performance

Design/style	Financial terms, e.g., discounts
Finish	Colour
Installation/fitting provided	Versatility/flexibility
Trade-in value	Size (product)
Price	Packaging
Delivery (on time)	Method of shipment

Life expectancy	Maintenance costs
Running costs	Ease of servicing
Brand name	Company reputation
Product/service image	Exclusivity
Administrative efficiency	Production strengths
Size of operations	Environmentally friendly

Patents/copyright	Safety features
Ease of use	Training provided
Compatible extras	Distribution network
Approval, e.g., BSI	Availability
Weight	Novelty value
After-sales servicing	Promotion

Quality of workforce	Guarantees/warranties
Competitor 1	Competitor 2
Competitor 3	Better
Same	Worse
Better	Same
Worse	Better

Same	Worse
Better	Same
Worse	Better
Same	Worse
Better	Same
Worse	Better

Same	Worse
Better	Same
Worse	Better
Same	Worse
Better	Same
Worse	Better

Same	Worse
Better	Same
Worse	Better
Same	Worse
Better	Same
Worse	Better

Same	Worse

Appendix 2
Further reading

For those wishing to explore further some of the areas touched upon in this book, the following could be useful.

Back, Ken and Kate, *Assertiveness at Work*, London: McGraw Hill 1982.

Berne, Eric, *The Games People Play*, New York: Grove Press 1969.

Camp, Robert C., *Benchmarking: The search for industry best practices that lead to superior performance*, Milwaukee, Wisc.: ASQC Quality Press 1989.

Christopher, Martin, *The Customer Service Planner*, Oxford: Butterworth-Heinemann 1991.

Christopher, Martin, Payne, Adrian and Ballantyne, David, *Relationship Marketing: Bringing quality, customer service and marketing together*, Oxford: Butterworth-Heinemann 1991.

Cook, Sarah, *Customer Care*, London: Kogan Page 1992.

Critlow, H.S. and S.J., *The Deming Guide to Quality and Competitive Position*, New York: Prentice Hall.

Harris, Thomas A., *I'm OK, You're OK*, London: Pan 1973 (an excellent book for anyone interested in understanding more about transactional analysis).

Hopson, Brian and Scally, Mike, *Twelve Steps to Success through Service*, Mercury Books 1991.

Lyles, Richard I., *Practical Management Problem Solving and Decision Making*, Bromley, Kent: Chartwell-Bratt 1982.

McDonald, Malcolm H.B., *Marketing Plans, How to prepare them: How to use them*, 2nd edn, Oxford: Butterworth-Heinemann 1989.

McDonald, Malcolm H.B. and Leppard, John, *Effective Industrial Selling*, Oxford: Butterworth-Heinemann 1988.

—— *The Marketing Audit*, Oxford: Butterworth-Heinemann 1991.

Majaro, Simon, *The Creative Marketer*, Oxford: Butterworth-Heinemann 1991.

Martin, William B., *Managing Quality Customer Service*, London: Kogan Page 1989.

Peel, Malcolm, *Customer Service: How to Achieve Total Customer Satisfaction*, London: Kogan Page 1988.

Peters, T. and Waterman, R., *In Search of Excellence*, New York: Harper & Row 1982.

Reichheld, F.F. and Sasser Jr, W.E., 'Zero defections: quality comes to services', *Harvard Business Review*, September–October 1990.

Appendix 3
Useful addresses associated with TQM

British Standards Institute
Business Development Unit
Linford Wood
Milton Keynes
Buckinghamshire
MK14 6LE

Tel: 0908 220908

The British Quality Foundation
Vigilant House
120 Wilton Road
London
SW1V 1JZ

Tel: 071 931 0607

The National Quality Information Centre
61 Southwark Street
London
SE1 1SB

Tel: 071 401 7227

Marketing Quality Assurance Ltd
The Brackens
London Road
Ascot
Berkshire
SL5 8BG

Tel: 0344 882400